World Politics, 3 (1950)

"The method of Communist Conquest: Hungary, 44-47

INTEGRATION AND COMMUNITY BUILDING
IN EASTERN EUROPE

INTEGRATION AND COMMUNITY BUILDING IN EASTERN EUROPE

Jan F. Triska, series editor

The German Democratic Republic
Arthur M. Hanhardt, Jr.

The Polish People's Republic
James F. Morrison

The Development of Socialist Yugoslavia
M. George Zaninovich

The People's Republic of Albania
Nicholas C. Pano

The Czechoslovak Socialist Republic
Zdenek Suda

The Socialist Republic of Rumania
Stephen Fischer-Galati

The Hungarian People's Republic
Bennett Kovrig

THE HUNGARIAN PEOPLE'S REPUBLIC

BENNETT KOVRIG

THE JOHNS HOPKINS PRESS

Baltimore and London

The Johns Hopkins Press, Baltimore, Maryland 21218
The Johns Hopkins Press Ltd., London

Library of Congress Catalog Card Number 72-101458
ISBN-0-8018-1126-0 (clothbound edition)
ISBN-0-8018-1128-7 (paperback edition)

Originally published, 1970
Johns Hopkins Paperbacks edition, 1970

FOREWORD

The Hungarian People's Republic is the seventh of a series of monographs dealing with integration and community building among the communist party states of Eastern Europe. These studies of East European countries are part of a larger program of studies of the communist system sponsored by Stanford University.

It seems appropriate here to outline the theoretical and methodological concepts that were developed for the series as a whole. The focus has been on the world communist movement as a system—its origins, development, and internal behavior. The major underlying assumption is that each communist party state has characteristics peculiar to it which predispose it toward varying degrees of cooperation, coordination, and integration with the others. We think that the present behavioral characteristics of the system can be traced to environmental, attitudinal, and systemic factors, and that we can learn a great deal from a comparative analysis of the process and degree of integration of each member state into the system of communist party states—whether, for example, the process involves force or consent, similar or shared institutions and codes of behavior, or whether integration is effective at elite levels and/or at lower levels as well, and so on.

The concept of political integration and community formation and maintenance is, as a focus of intellectual curiosity and investigation, as old as the study of politics. The mushrooming of supranational integrational movements since World War II has given a considerable new impetus to the old curiosity and has changed the emphasis of the investigations. Social scientists who in the last two decades have been building a general theory of political integration—whether on a subnational, national, or supranational level— have been perhaps less concerned with the philosophical content of the concept of integration than with discovering operational indicators that would endow the concept with empirical meaning and allow the theory to be tested for validity and reliability. The principal centers of their inquiry have been two broad, independent variables, *interaction* and *attitude*. Although in most cases investigated separately, interaction and attitude are assumed to combine to constitute a *community*, the *objective* of the *process* of integration.

The principal subjects of inquiry have been *transactions* across the boundaries of state units and *attitude formation* within the states. The theorists stipulate that numerous transactions are necessary for political integration and they postulate that the density of transactions among the units indicates their relationship to one another. The flow of mail and telephone traffic; trade; aid; exchange of tourists, officials, and migrants; cultural exchange of persons and communications; newspapers, periodicals, and book sales and translations; radio, TV, and motion picture exchange; mutual treaties and agreements; common organizations and conferences—these are the kinds of indicators that, measured and plotted over time, should demonstrate the direction of integrational trends and developments.

With reference to *attitude formation,* theorists have been more concerned with the process of integration than with its results (conditions) within the individual states. The pertinent literature yields relatively little on this subject. In *Nationalism and Social Communication,* Karl Deutsch argues that it may be fruitful to study two sets of persons within a unit of analysis: those "mobilized" for integrational communications and those "assimilated" into the new and larger unit. If those assimilated multiply at a more rapid rate than those mobilized, then "assimilation" is gaining and "community is growing faster than society."

At present, enormous problems are involved in studying the *results* of the integration process in communist countries. It is difficult to assess attitudes because of the great sensitivity of officials and decision-makers, and it is either difficult or impossible to get reliable aggregate and survey data. This informational problem makes it correspondingly difficult to develop a general theory of integration or to make systematic comparative analyses. We have therefore been compelled to rely on indicators of degrees and trends, indicators which depend considerably on subjective judgment and inference.

Although the data available are uneven in quality and quantity, our approach has been rigorous and systematic. Each author was asked to examine the country under review with reference to five historical periods: (1) the pre-communist stage before the country became a party state and hence a member of the system; (2) the period of the communists' consolidation of power after World War II when the states of Eastern Europe entered the system; (3) the subsequent era of repression and rigid controls; (4) the period of relaxed controls following Stalin's death; (5) the last ten years. For each of these periods, as appropriate, the author was asked to identify and analyze the phenomena relevant to this country's integration into the system, its ecological-physical features, its demographic structure, belief system, social system, degree of autonomy, its dependence on other states, and its hopes, needs, and expectations with regard to integration and development. Within these broad confines, each author was asked to emphasize the periods and events with the greatest significance for the integrational development of the country in question. It is our feeling that a more rigid set of prescriptions would have been self-defeating in view of our objectives and the exploratory nature of our undertaking.

The present study examines principally those aspects of the behavior of the Hungarian People's Republic which are relevant to integration and community formation with its neighbors and socialist friends in Eastern Europe. True, Bennett Kovrig's narrative is such that it lends itself also as a useful introduction to any student of Hungary. But the backbone of the study is the Soviet-Hungarian relationship: "By and large [since the fall of Khrushchev] the Hungarian leadership has been consistent in its pursuit of a centrist course that deviates only marginally from the international policies of the CPSU," argues Professor Kovrig. "Hungary's alignment with Moscow was never put in question. . . . Kádár's calculated allegiance to Moscow as well as his inclination to liberalize cautiously and to moderate interparty conflicts" have been characteristic of Hungarian behavior.

Like the other monographs in the series, this study is divided into five historical parts. Each period is discussed in terms of the changes that took place in the environment of the Hungarian socioeconomic-political system—both in other parts of the communist system and in the rest of the world—and is analyzed for the most significant domestic changes relevant to Hungary's integration into the system. In addition, there is a discussion in each period of the changes that took place in the form and degree of Hungary's integration into the system, the costs and benefits for various segments of the Hungarian population, and the major conflicts between Hungary and the rest of the system resulting from the nature of the integration during the given period.

The series is an intellectual product of many creative minds. In addition to the authors of the individual monographs—in this case, Professor Bennett Kovrig, Department of Political Economy, University of Toronto—I would like to thank especially Professor David D. Finley of The Colorado College for his original contribution and assistance, and John Gallman of the Washington office of The Johns Hopkins Press for his patient and sustained cooperation.

JAN F. TRISKA

Institute of Political Studies
Stanford University

CONTENTS

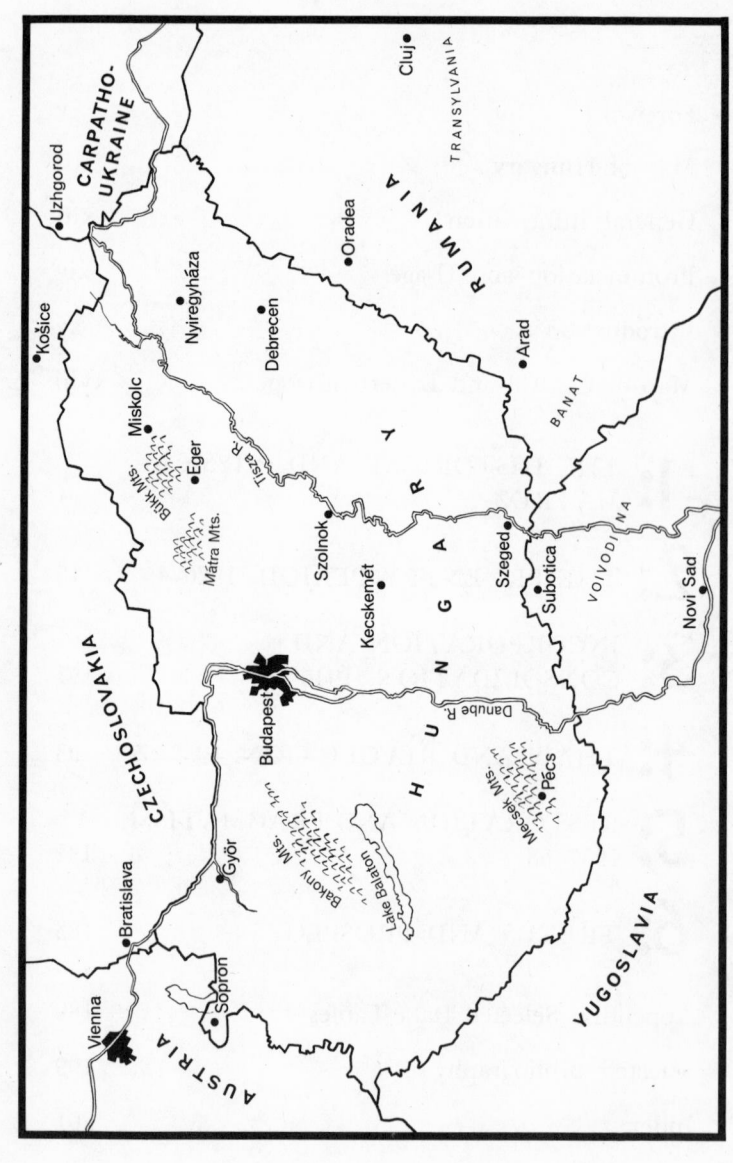

The Hungarian People's Republic
Magyar Népköztársaság

Area: 35,919 square miles (93,030 sq. km.)
Population: 10,236,000 (1968)
Population density: 285 per square mile (1968)
Major cities   *Population* (1968)

Budapest	1,985,000
Miskolc	178,000
Debrecen	155,000
Pécs	139,000
Szeged	121,000

Birth rate: 14.6 per 1,000 population (1967)
Death rate: 10.7 per 1,000 population (1967)
Natural increase: 3.9 per 1,000 population (1967)
Infant mortality: 37.0 per 1,000 live births (1967)
Marriages: 9.4 per 1,000 population (1967)
Divorces: 2.1 per 1,000 population (1967)
Literacy (ten years of age and older): 98.4 per cent (1968)
School enrollment (1967-68)

Kindergarten	196,973
Primary school	1,331,079
Secondary schools	351,186
Postsecondary institutions	83,938

Publishing

Books	47.8 million copies (1967)
Newspapers and periodicals	992.0 million copies (1967)

Communications

Radio receivers	242 per 1,000 population (1967)
Television receivers	114 per thousand population (1967)
Telephones (excluding extensions)	33 per 1,000 population (1967)

Transportation (1967)
Automobiles   144,601

	Passengers	*Goods*
Rail	562,411,000	117,651,000 tons
Water	4,369,000	9,383,000 tons
Road	404,027,000	263,273,000 tons
Air	242,000	8,000 tons
Pipeline		6,350,000 tons

Usually classified in the Finno-Ugrian group and distantly related to Finnish and Estonian (and also, apparently, to the extinct Sumerian tongue), the Hungarian language is spoken by some thirteen million people in Eastern Europe. In pronunciation the stress is invariably on the first syllable. It should be noted that in a Hungarian context the patronym precedes the given name. The following is a partial guide to the pronunciation of personal and place names cited in this monograph:

Letter	Equivalent	Example
a	*h*a*ll	Buda
á	c*ar*	András
c	ca*ts*	Bence
cs	*ch*erub	Pécs
e	br*ea*d	Ferenc
é	l*a*te	Béla
g	*g*arden	Gábor
gy	*d'y*ou	Gyula
i	s*i*n	István
j	*y*es	János
ly	mil*l*ion	Károly
ö	h*u*rry	György
ő	p*ea*rl	Ernő
o	l*o*ss	Lajos
ó	l*ow*	Miklós
s	*sh*ield	Pest
sz	*s*ee	László
ty	*t*une	Mátyás
u	wh*o*	Gyula
ü	F*ü*hrer	Bükk
z	*z*ebra	Géza
zs	lei*s*ure	Zsuzsa

INTRODUCTION

Thirteen years have passed since the autumn of 1956, when for thirteen days the world watched in disbelief as the Hungarian revolution progressed in the midst of nationalistic euphoria toward ultimate and perhaps inevitable defeat. In its initial stages the revolution appeared to be an early manifestation of the phenomenon of polycentrism; its failure provided an indication, which has since been reasserted in Czechoslovakia, of the limits of voluntarism within the Soviet sphere. Subsequently there arose two schools of thought among students of that sphere. The first tended to view Eastern Europe as a static and undifferentiated appendage of the Soviet Union, its party leaders as Pavlovian pawns of the Kremlin, much as they had been in Stalin's day. The other, and increasingly predominant, school saw in the signs of functional (and, more rarely, structural) liberalization evidence that the system was undergoing an inexorable, historical process of change toward a state of democratic compatibility and consensual interpedendence. Recent developments in Eastern Europe and the Soviet Union invite a reappraisal of these competing orthodoxies. With the exception of Yugoslavia, whose apostasy has survived all integrative pressures, and despite Rumania's economic nationalism, subsystem autonomy remains closely circumscribed; on the other hand, variations in the patterns of change, inspired by intrinsically national considerations, suggest that the model of a Stalinist monolith is no longer applicable. As long as the Soviet Union retains its existing social and political structure and its claim to be the fountainhead of a universal ideology (and there is little indication of permissiveness in the adherence of the present hard-line leadership to these tenets), the party states of Eastern Europe—again expecting Yugoslavia—must be viewed as largely submissive clients whose options in internal and external policy are tangible but qualitatively limited.

Focusing on Hungary's role within the system, this monograph seeks to analyze both the internal dynamics of change and the systemic parameters within which change occurs. In addition, since Hungary's participation in the system was externally imposed as a consequence of the postwar balance of power and was only marginally the outcome of indigenous factors, an attempt is made in the first two chapters to sketch those historical constants which remain relevant today. Subsequent chapters explore, within a broadly chronological framework, the most salient aspects of political and socioeconomic change and their systemic significance. Apart from the 1956 conflagration, Hungary as a party state has been among the most loyal to the Soviet Union, but, as will be seen, this loyalty has not precluded economic and other experiments that reflect the particular needs and environmental characteristics of the country. While integration is a relative concept, Hungary unquestionably forms part of a distinct regional system that has historical as well as ideological roots, and this study therefore concentrates on the nature of the integrative process, on its implications for Hungary, and on its future prospects; economic integration, despite its slow progress, has brought certain benefits to Hungary without removing the latter's desire to compete on the less protected world market. Finally, it is hoped that the analysis also provides some general insights into the social, economic, and political consequences for a small nation-state of membership in the sphere of influence of a superpower.

In the preparation of this monograph, the sustained encouragement of the series' editor, Professor Jan F. Triska, has been invaluable. Thanks are also due to Mr. R. F. Thompson for his fine cartographic contribution.

BENNETT KOVRIG

Department of Political Economy
University of Toronto

1: THE HISTORICAL AND PHYSICAL MATRIX

Determinism in its historical and geographical forms has frequently surfaced in the national consciousness of Hungarians, and conceptions of Hungary as being one of the "historical" nations of East Central Europe and mistress of the Carpathian Basin have exerted an integrative as well as disruptive influence in the area up to the time of her entry into the communist system. Any analysis of her contemporary political culture and its systemic implications which fails to take into account these factors runs the risk of positivistic distortion. Consequently, this chapter aims to provide an overview of the multifaceted developments that brought Hungary to the beginning of the pre-entry period.

The Realm of St. Stephen

It was one of the more remarkable mass migrations in human history that brought the Magyars into the heart of Europe toward the end of the ninth century. The previously constant movement of this nomadic people makes conclusive ethnic identification difficult; the orthodox classification of the Magyars in the Ural-Altaic group (suggesting their geographical origins

1

around the mountains of the same name) has been qualified by recent research that points to a putative Sumerian ancestry.[1] Whatever may be the outcome of such ethnogenic speculations, history records that the seven tribes—numbering in all perhaps a quarter of a million and led by their chieftain Árpád—made their way westward after unsuccessful battles with the Pechenegs along the north shore of the Black Sea and crossed the Carpathian range in the winter of 895–96.

The entrance of the Magyars into the Danubian Basin can be characterized less as an invasion than as settlement. The areas west of the Danube and southeast of the Carpathians once had been the Roman provinces of Pannonia and Dacia, and in later centuries various nomadic peoples, notably the Huns and the Avars, established a transitory presence on the central plains. In 896, however, the latter area was claimed by neither the German nor the Byzantine Empire, although it was flanked north and south by the semi-independent Moravian and Croatian states. Thus it was with relative ease that the Magyars established their dominion in the middle of the basin, a dominion which through their alliance with the ethnically related Szeklers extended to the remote passes of the Transylvanian Alps. They brought with them a rudimentary runic script, a basically undifferentiated social structure founded on the clan, and a reputation for horsemanship which was spread through Europe by raids ranging from Bremen to Constantinople. Decisive defeat by the German emperor Otto I at Augsburg in 955 ended the Magyar raids and ushered in a period of internal consolidation.

[1] See Ida Bobula, *Origin of the Hungarian Nation* (Gainesville, Fla., 1966). Evidence demonstrating that the Sumerian culture was implanted in the Carpathian Basin centuries before Árpád's arrival is advanced by Dr. Sándor Nagy, *A magyar nép kialakulásának töténete* (Buenos Aires, 1968).

The contest between Rome and Byzantium for the spiritual allegiance of the Magyars culminated in the victory of the former in 975, when Árpád's great-grandson, Géza, formally joined the Western church. This alignment was immeasurably strengthened by one of the key events in Hungary's history when in the year 1000 Pope Sylvester II granted a crown and apostolic cross to King Stephen I. Under the reign of Stephen peace with Hungary's neighbors prevailed, while internally the country was organized into counties and benefited from the civilizing influence of the Benedictine order; the social structure consisted of the "national community" of freemen (descendants of the original Magyars) and the politically inactive non-Magyar immigrants, as well as a declining number of slaves. The realm of St. Stephen, a supranational concept endowed by the Magyars with mystical significance, encompassed Transylvania as well as the associate state of Croatia following the acquisition by King Kálmán of the Croatian crown in 1097. By 1200 the population of Hungary, excluding Croatia, numbered some two million people.

Physiography

The physical features of the national kingdom are worthy of note, for, apart from periodic invasions and partitions, they coincided with subsequent state boundaries until the end of World War I. Although natural boundaries have lost some of their strategic significance, for many centuries they were an important factor in delineating and facilitating the defense of Hungary. The north and northeast frontiers followed the line of the Carpathians, the Transylvanian Alps marked the southeastern outposts, while in the west the borders extended to the foothills of the Austrian Alps. The Danube, running west-east and then north-south, bisects the bowl enclosed by these ranges, and forms the nucleus of the drainage basin before it leaves the central lowlands. Most of these lowlands—the Carpathian Basin—are flat, featureless steppe. East of the Danube lies the Alföld, or Great Plain, broken only by the Tisza River; the Dunántúl, or Transdanubia, lying west of the Danube and north of the Sava and Drava rivers, has a more varied topography that includes Lake Balaton, covering 160 square miles, as well as lesser mountain ranges north and south of the lake, with the highest peak under 3,000 feet. A third area, the northern upland, acquired significance following the 1919 partitions; it is characterized by the Mátra and Bükk mountain ranges, the former being a southerly extension of the Carpathians.

The economy of the Alföld has been dictated by its flatness and its fertile soil; apart from pockets of grassland, or *puszta,* suitable for livestock-grazing, it was for centuries given over to extensive agriculture and produced chiefly bread grains and cereals. Irrigation and the reclamation of marshlands contributed to diversification, and the last century has seen the beginnings of viticulture and rice production. Viticulture had earlier beginnings in the northern upland, where the Tokaj wine originated, and around the shores of Lake Balaton. The northern end of Transdanubia, known as the Little Plain, has had an agricultural economy similar to the Alföld. Indeed, at the turn of the nineteenth century close to 90 per cent of Hungary's population owed its living to agriculture. The extractive industries were limited to the mining of some precious metals in Transylvania and northern

Hungary; coal-mining, primarily in the Mecsek Mountains near Pécs, grew as an industry in the 1800's, while the extraction of bauxite, uranium, and oil materialized only in the present century. Imperial design as well as ecological factors contributed to Hungary's role as Central Europe's breadbasket and to her slow rate of industrialization. Her physical environment and geographical situation had even more far-reaching consequences. The Hungarian plain, astride the main waterway linking the Balkans with Western Europe, was strategically important not only as a commercial link between East and West but also as an invasion route that was taken by the Mongols in the thirteenth century and by the Turks in the sixteenth century, in both cases with devastating consequences. With the expansion of trade in the nineteenth century, Hungary's access to the Adriatic through the port of Fiume (now Rijeka) also acquired strategic significance, but the Treaty of Trianon in 1920 reduced the country to its present landlocked position.[2]

From the Ottoman to the Habsburg Empire

The Mongol invasion of 1241 left Hungary weakened not only politically, particularly vis à vis Austria, but also physically, from the enormous loss of life, and the process of recolonization undertaken by King Béla further reduced the numerical strength of the Magyars. The internal social structure was also altered by the increased power of the magnates, landowners who acquired feudal power in exchange for their participation in the military apparatus of the postinvasion

[2] See Ernst C. Helmreich, ed., *Hungary* (New York, 1957), chap. 3, and Márton Pécsi and Béla Sárfalvi, *The Geography of Hungary* (Budapest, 1964).

period. Despite the Golden Bull of 1222, which like the Magna Charta had granted to the gentry certain rights at the expense of royal prerogative, the power of the magnates was maintained and extended through their allegiance to successive dynasties.[3]

The year 1301 saw the last of the Árpád line pass away, and subsequently only two indigenous kings came to rule over Hungary. Nevertheless, some of the so-called foreign kings reigned with notable success. The country flourished under the Angevin Louis the Great, who extended Hungarian suzerainty over Wallachia, Dalmatia, and other dependencies, fostered the development of towns and commerce, and founded the University of Pécs in 1367. Under the following reigns, however, the expanding Ottoman Empire reached the southern borders of Hungary, and it fell upon the latter to defend Christian Europe from the designs of the infidels. In these numerous clashes the ruler of Transylvania, János Hunyadi, played a leading role, ultimately as regent for the Austrian boy-king Ladislas, and he inflicted a heavy defeat on the Turks at Belgrade in 1456. Two years later the Hungarian nobility, taking advantage of an interregnum, elected as their king Hunyadi's son, Matthias Corvinus. With Matthias the Renaissance penetrated Hungary; the arts flourished, accommodation was reached with the Bohemian leader Giskra and Emperor Frederick of Austria, and the administration of the country was streamlined, without, however, any transferance of power to the Diet. Following Matthias' death, the Jagiello dynasty, already ruling Bohemia, was extended to Hungary. Meanwhile, the social structure remained essentially unchanged. With the jurist Werbőczy's compilation of laws (the 1514 *Tripartitum*) the gentry saw their rights reaf-

[3] See Elemér Hantos, *The Magna Carta of the English and of the Hungarian Constitution* (London, 1904).

firmed as to both their legal equality and their participation in the Diet, but the magnates continued to prevail. In contrast the peasants had seen their already minimal rights whittled away, and in 1514 a crusading army revolted under the leadership of György Dózsa; the revolt ended in a bloodbath and led to even more repressive measures.

The trials of peasants and gentry faded into insignificance when renewed Turkish pressures culminated in the defeat of the Hungarian army in 1526 at the Battle of Mohács. King Louis fell in battle, and the problems of succession were added to the threat of invasion. Most of Hungary's nobility favored the ruler of Transylvania, John Zápolyai, while Ferdinand pressed the Habsburgs' claim. Buda fell to the Turks in 1541, and for the next century and a half Hungary was divided into three parts: a strip in the northwest, "Royal Hungary," remained under Habsburg rule; the central area was incorporated into the Ottoman Empire; and in the east, Transylvania maintained an uneasy and often qualified independence from both empires. A further complicating factor arose with the spread of the Reformation in Hungary; it developed strong roots, particularly in Transylvania, but in Royal Hungary the Counter Reformation of the Habsburgs and their loyal magnates deepened the religious cleavage. When the Turks were finally driven from Hungary (Buda was recaptured in 1686), they left behind a country devastated and depopulated, devoid of any strength to oppose the dynastic ambitions of the Habsburgs. The Diet of 1687 ratified the latter's hereditary rights, and in one form or another Austrian rule continued to prevail in Hungary until the end of World War I.

Early revolts against Vienna's harsh rule and religious persecution were led by Ferenc Rákóczi in 1697 and for several years thereafter, and they were instrumental in extracting certain palliatives: Hungary was to be ruled by a Palatine—advised by a council and the Diet sitting in Pozsony (now Bratislava)—and with due respect for her national rights and body of laws. The reign of Maria Theresa brought further marginal improvements, as well as a flowering of the baroque culture fostered mainly by the wealthy magnates. The power of the diets in Pozsony and Transylvania was limited, however, to the ratification of imperial policies. These policies aimed to Germanize Hungary and imposed discriminatory tariffs that effectively prevented industrialization outside Austria and Bohemia; the *urbarium* of 1767 rationalized the status and obligations of the peasants, but to the extent that this weakened the position of the landowning nobility it only strengthened the latter's opposition to the crown. The policy that had the most far-reaching consequences was the organized settlement of areas depopulated by centuries of warfare. The Vlach (Rumanian) elements in Transylvania were now more numerous, and their settlements proliferated particularly in the area between Transylvania and inner Hungary known as the Partium; southern Slavs, Slovaks, Ruthenes, and Germans also grew in number, the first and the last chiefly in southern Hungary and the Bánát, the others in the north and northeast. In the towns, Germans and Jews became a significant ethnic element.

Reform, Revolution, and Compromise

By the turn of the nineteenth century, Magyar nationalism was undergoing a revival of such proportions that Vienna felt obliged to offer concessions in exchange for financial support of imperial wars. The Diet of 1825, convoked after a lapse of thirteen years, ushered in a "reform era" that saw the spread of the Magyar language in administration and education and a concomitant revitalization of the national culture in all its aspects. Count István Széchenyi, a moderate reformer, became widely known for his expositions of the social, economic, and political shortcomings besetting Hungary, and he urged upon his countrymen a program of modernization. Lajos Kossuth, a member of the landless gentry, recommended even greater reforms in personal liberties and the franchise, reforms that marked him as a social radical where Széchenyi had been a mere progressive; moreover, he outbid the latter in a more critical direction by calling for Hungary's national self-determination and sovereignty. Inevitably, this burgeoning nationalism affected the minorities as well, and the Croats, then the other Slavs, as well as the Saxons and Rumanians in Transylvania, voiced demands for linguistic and political rights. Initially these demands proved ineffectual because of Metternich's tactical preference for conciliating the more powerful Magyars, but they were reasserted with a vengeance once the empire crumbled.

The revolution that broke out in Vienna in March, 1848, provided Kossuth with his opportunity for pressing the demands of the nationalist opposition, and Emperor Ferdinand consented to the formation of a responsible Hungarian cabinet headed by Count Lajos Batthyány and to Hungary's union with Transylvania. These reforms proved to be short-lived, however. Unrest among the national minorities found its strongest expression in Croatia, and an army, led by Count Josip Jellašič and encouraged by Vienna, invaded Hungary Following a political consolidation under the new emperor, Francis Joseph I, the faltering Croatians were joined by an Austrian army, but the Hungarian National Guard inflicted heavy defeats upon them. The revolutionary war of 1848–49 provided Hungary with a number of national heroes, notably the poet Sándor Petőfi and the Polish general Bem, and, indeed, early successes added to the aura of Kossuth, who had become governor. But the Concert of Europe prevailed in the end, and with the help of Russian armies dispatched by Czar Nicholas I the Austrians crushed the revolt.

The years following the revolution were marked by oppressive military rule and passive resistance. The moderate group which urged the latter course was led by Ferenc Deák, and his pressures, in conjunction with the reverses that Austria had suffered in her foreign ventures, brought about the establishment of the Dual Monarchy through the Compromise of 1867. Hungary became self-governing except for matters relating to foreign relations and defense, which remained under joint administration; a Hungarian-Croatian compromise maintained Croatia's semi-independence, and Transylvania was incorporated. This political structure remained in force until the Great War.

Social and Economic Patterns

The political stabilization in the postcompromise era ushered in a period of peace that did not, however, foster the resolution of those problems of modernization which beset all of Europe. A franchise that even in 1910 extended to only 8 per cent of the population effectively limited political participation; the reins of political power remained in the hands of the magnates and the middle nobility. Demographic and economic changes, on the other hand, led to demands that surpassed the capabilities of the various administrations headed by Deák, Gyula Andrássy, and Kálmán Tisza.[4] The population had risen from 13,000,000 in 1850 to 20,886,487 by 1910, creating a surplus that could scarcely be accommodated by the slow rate of industrialization—and this in spite of vast programs of land reclamation. Urbanization brought about a decline in the agricultural population to 64.5 per cent by 1910, but, while legislation in 1848 had freed the peasants from the old feudal obligations and had enlarged the small freeholder class, close to half of the total rural population remained landless; in contrast, almost one-third of the country was given over to the estates of fewer than 4,000 proprietors. Thus an agricultural proletariat arose whose impoverished state led to mass emigration at the turn of the century and sparked a Western-oriented populist literary movement that included the poet Endre Ady. The state's promotion of industrial development was not accompanied by adequate social legislation, and the Social Democratic movement's growth in the 1890's represented only modest progress in the direction of social mobilization.

These socioeconomic problems were overshadowed by the pressures of nationalism and national minorities, pressures that predominated in the political culture of the postcompromise era as well as in the subsequent interwar period. The Nationalities Act of 1868 had

[4] A concise account is given in C. A. Macartney, *Hungary: A Short History* (Chicago, 1962), pp. 193ff. The best general history in Hungarian is still that of Bálint Hóman and Gyula Szekfű, *Magyar Történet*, 5 vols. (Budapest, 1935-36).

11

sanctioned the use of minority languages in education and the churches and to a more limited extent in local administrations, while maintaining Hungarian as the official language. Neither the Magyars nor the minorities were entirely satisfied with this arrangement.

Imbued with the concept of the indivisible realm of St. Stephen and with the nationalism that was sweeping Europe in the latter half of the nineteenth century, the Magyar ruling classes launched a program of Magyarization which, notably through the Education Act of 1879, sought to assimilate the minority elements. The program achieved only limited success, both in the sphere of behavioral assimilation and in terms of structural integration. Serbs, Rumanians, and Croats were most successful in preserving their national identities, while Slovaks and Germans proved more amenable, the Germans in particular contributing to the growth of the new urban middle class and to the state administration. A further significant alteration in the social structure was occasioned by the influx of Jews, who by 1900 accounted for close to 5 per cent of the total and for a much higher proportion of the urban population. Their increasingly dominant role in entrepreneurial, intellectual, and politically radical activities fed the flames of an anti-Semitism that previously had not been prevalent in Hungarian life.

Magyarization was successful in the urban areas. But, excluding Croatia, only a little more than half of the Hungarian population had claimed Magyar as its mother tongue by 1900. Consequently, the centrifugal forces exerted by the national minorities remained as a disruptive factor in the social and political system of pre–World War I Hungary. The problem of national self-determination in the Carpathian Basin appeared well-nigh insoluble in view of the ethnic mosaic.[5] From exile, Lajos Kossuth belatedly recognized this fact as well as the perils of fragmentation: "Each nation of the lower Danube—even if it should succeed in gathering around itself its racial relations now belonging elsewhere—could form, in the best case, only a second-rate state, the independence of which would incessantly be in jeopardy, and which state would necessarily be subjected to foreign influences."[6] His recommendation—later echoed by František Palacký and Oscar Jászi—was that a Danubian confederation be set up "according to the old example given by the Swiss." But the warning fell on deaf ears; the Great War brought about a power vacuum in Eastern Europe which ultimately turned it into a military and ideological battleground.

[5] See Robert A. Kann, *The Multinational Empire: Nationalism and National Reform in the Habsburg Monarchy, 1848–1918* (New York, 1950), and Oscar Jászi, *The Dissolution of the Habsburg Monarchy* (Chicago, 1929).

[6] Cited in Béla Talbot Kardos, "From Kossuth's Unknown Federalist Papers," *Studies for a New Central Europe,* 1, no. 1 (1963) : 71.

2: THE PRE-ENTRY PERIOD, 1920–45

The forces of social discontent and of Magyar and minority nationalism, latent for many years, all came to a climax in the last days of the Great War, when defeat appeared imminent and the Bolshevik Revolution sent its shockwaves across Europe.[1] In October, 1918, a leader of the Party of Independence, Count Mihály Károlyi, was brought to power at the head of a coalition of independents, radicals, and Social Democrats, and he proceeded to abrogate the Compromise of 1867 and to proclaim a republic of which he then became the provisional president. Károlyi's first task was to negotiate a *modus vivendi* with the nationalities in a new democratic Hungary. The fact that he failed in this task is a mark of the extreme nationalism that had struck roots among the minorities, for the latter now demanded outright secession. France's wartime diplomacy had worked to strengthen the aspirations of Czechs, Rumanians, and Serbs with promises of self-determination if they assisted in the defeat of the Entente Powers,[2] and accordingly armies from all three

[1] A rather hyperbolic account of the labor movement during World War I is given by Erzsébet Andics, *A magyar munkásmozgalom az 1914–18as világháboru alatt* (Budapest, 1950).

[2] For the Entente-Rumanian agreement of 1916, see C. A. Macartney, *Hungary and Her Successors* (Oxford, 1937), p. 275.

groups moved in to occupy large sections of Hungarian territory. The Western Powers, oblivious to Károlyi's withdrawal from the Dual Monarchy, ordered him to evacuate these territories, including all of Transylvania, and turn them over to Czech and Rumanian administration. Unable to negotiate with his interlocutors and with no time to implement reforms that might have consolidated his regime internally, Károlyi resigned.[3]

The end of Károlyi's interregnum brought to the fore the more radical element in his government, the Social Democrats, who themselves rapidly abdicated effective power to a handful of workers' and soldiers' councils led by the man Lenin had chosen to bring the Bolshevik Revolution to Hungary, Béla Kun. The latter's promise to liberate the occupied territories with the help of the Red Army (which in the event never became involved) brought him a modicum of popular support, but his short-lived attempts at social and economic reforms and the terrorist activities of his henchman, Tibor Szamuely rapidly alienated not only the middle classes and the peasantry but also the urban workers and the Social Democrats.[4] Following initial successes against the Czechs, Kun failed to hold back the Rumanians and the latter occupied Budapest while Kun fled to Vienna, thus bringing to an end the Soviet Republic.[5]

[3] His own interpretation of the events can be found in Michael Károlyi, *Faith Without Illusion* (London, 1956); cf. Tibor Hajdu, *Az 1918-as magyarországi polgáridemokratikus forradalom* (Budapest, 1968).

[4] See R. L. Tőkés, *Béla Kun and the Hungarian Soviet Republic* (New York, 1967); cf. F. T. Zsuppán, "The Early Activities of the Hungarian Communist Party, 1918–1919," *The Slavonic and East European Review*, 43, no. 101 (1965): 314–34, and Katalin Petrák and György Milei, eds., *A Magyar Tanácsköztársaság szociálpolitikája* (Budapest, 1959).

[5] For his relations with the Entente Powers, see Alfred D.

In the meantime a provisional, anti-Bolshevik government had been formed in the southern provincial city of Szeged, which dispatched its military commander, Admiral Miklós Horthy, to Budapest, whence the Rumanians had withdrawn after a period of widespread looting. With the sanction of the Entente Powers a caretaker government came into office on November 24, 1919, and set out to establish the foundation of a new and popularly based political system. The thankless task of negotiating a peace treaty devolved upon this new government, although the negotiations took the form of a *Diktat* that was in effect a travesty of the Wilsonian principles of self-determination which allegedly inspired the peacemakers at Versailles.[6]

Demographic and Territorial Changes

The Treaty of Trianon, signed on June 4, 1920, had incalculable social, economic, and political consequences not only for Hungary but for all of Eastern Europe, and accordingly they will be reflected throughout this chapter. In terms of territory, Hungary was reduced to 28.6 per cent of her pre-Trianon area. Of the latter area, 31.5 per cent, comprising Transylvania and part of the Bánát, was awarded to Rumania; 19.6 per cent was transferred to the new state of Yugoslavia;

Low, *The Soviet Republic and the Paris Peace Conference* (Philadelphia, 1963), and F. T. Zsuppán, "The Hungarian Soviet Republic and the British Military Representatives, April-June, 1919," *The Slavonic and East European Review,* 47, no. 108 (1969) : 198–218.

[6] See Ferenc Deák, *Hungary at the Paris Peace Conference* (New York, 1942) ; cf. Macartney, *Hungary and Her Successors,* and R. W. Seton-Watson, *Treaty Revision and the Hungarian Frontiers* (London, 1934).

Czechoslovakia received 18.9 per cent, including the cities of Pozsony (Bratislava) and Kassa (Košice); and smaller territories were incorporated into Austria, Italy, and Poland. The much-vaunted geographical and economic unity of the Carpathian Basin clearly had not carried much weight at the bargaining tables; the new Hungary was a predominantly flat land in the middle of the basin, devoid of any natural boundaries.

It might be argued that geographical advantages had rightly been overridden by considerations of ethnic homogeneity and national self-determination. Unfortunately, the latter criteria were applied so as to benefit solely the successor states, which absorbed more than 13 million of the prewar population of Hungary. Of these, 1,704,851 persons of Magyar mother tongue went to Rumania, 1,063,020 to Czechoslovakia, 547,735 to Yugoslavia, and 26,183 to Austria for a total of 3,219,579 extraterritorial Hungarians.[7] Conceivably, an additional hypothesis could be advanced to justify these transfers: that the Magyar elements were so dispersed throughout the successors' annexed territories that the multi-ethnic mosaic of the successor states would be analogous to the composition of post-Trianon Hungary. However, Magyars lived in homogeneous settlements across from, and contiguous with, the Trianon borders in Slovakia and in the Bánát, while the following figures indicate the strength of minorities as a proportion of the total population of East European countries in the interwar period:[8]

[7] C. A. Macartney, *October Fifteenth: A History of Modern Hungary, 1929–1945*, 2 vols. (Edinburgh, 1956-57), 1 : 4; cf. Harold Temperley, "How the Hungarian Frontiers Were Drawn," *Foreign Affairs*, 6 (1928) : 432–47.

[8] Thomas T. Hammond, "Nationalism and National Minorities in Eastern Europe," *Journal of International Affairs*, 20, no. 1 (1966) : 17. The reannexations noted below brought the proportion of minorities in Hungary up to 22.5 per cent.

Hungary (1920), 10 per cent

Czechoslovakia (1930, not counting Slovaks as a minority), 33 per cent

Rumania (1930), 28 per cent

Yugoslavia (1921, not counting Croats as a minority), 17 per cent

Clearly, whatever the injustices that characterized the minorities policies of Hungarian regimes in the post-compromise era, the Treaty of Trianon was essentially a punitive peace settlement which lacked a realistic demographic and ethnic foundation.

Post-Trianon Hungary, then, covered an area of 35,893 square miles (compared to 125,641 square miles in 1914, including Croatia), with a population of 7,990,202 (compared to the 1914 figure of 20,886,000).[9] The natural rate of growth was fairly high in the inter-war period, averaging 8.7 per cent between 1920 and 1930, and in the latter year the population reached 8,688,319, with a relatively high density of 242 persons per square mile.

As a consequence of political maneuvers that will be outlined later, Hungary regained some territory and population on the eve of World War II. By the first Vienna Award of November, 1938, 4,640 square miles of Slovakia, containing a Magyar majority, were re-annexed; four months later, Hungary reoccupied Ruthenia (4,670 square miles); in August, 1940, the second Vienna Award returned 16,650 square miles of northern Transylvania, again with a Magyar majority; and in the following year Hungary reoccupied the

[9] Helmreich, *Hungary*, pp. 46ff. Due to recalculations, the figure for the present area of Hungary is higher than that for the Trianon area, despite the net loss of the "Bratislava bridge-head."

Bácska (the Yugoslav Voivodina), with an area of 4,440 square miles. The aggregate result of these changes left Hungary in 1941 with an area of 66,315 square miles and a population of 14,683,323. The ethnic composition of Hungary's population became increasingly homogeneous up to the time of the first Vienna Award, largely as a result of repatriations. In 1930, 92.1 per cent were Magyar; the Germans, with 5.5 per cent, remained as the largest minority. As regards the religious variable, despite the Counter Reformation, Protestantism had maintained itself through the centuries (with particular vigor in Transylvania) and the Roman Catholic church never became as inclusive as it did in Poland. Even the ruling classes numbered many Protestant families. According to the 1930 census, 64.9 per cent of the population professed to be Roman Catholic, 27 per cent Calvinist or Lutheran, and 5.1 per cent Jewish; there were also lesser numbers of Greek Catholics, Greek Orthodox, and Unitarians.

In sum, Hungary's demographic profile in the pre-entry period presented the picture of a densely populated, ethnically homogeneous, and predominantly Christian nation.

The Belief System and Political Movements

Among the predominant values in Hungary in the pre-entry period were irredentist nationalism, counter-revolutionary conservatism, and a Western cultural orientation; a national brand of populism also struck strong roots, although it was hampered by a profound urban-rural cleavage. All of these values, singly or in conjunction, found expression in the various political movements and cultural manifestation of the day.

The primary consensual element in the political culture of the nation, and that which exerted internally the strongest integrative influence, was opposition to the Trianon dismemberment. As the foremost Western historian of Hungary observed, "the desire and determination to achieve some revision of this Treaty were nation-wide in Hungary throughout the entire period."[10] The slogan *"nem, nem, soha"* ("no, no, never") acquired widespread currency not only among the old élites but across all socioeconomic divisions. Numerous secret societies and paramilitary organizations were formed in the 1920's, some of which had a strictly irredentist ideology; others were characterized by a tinge of right radicalism, a blending of anti-bolshevism and implicit revisionism that was known as the "Szeged idea," named after the city where the various nationalist and conservative elements had gathered under the Soviet Republic. Ultimately, an organization called the *Társadalmi Egyesületek Szövetsége* (Federation of Social Associations) was formed to oversee the activities of the proliferation of patriotic associations. Some of the latter, notably the *Vitézi Rend* (Order of Heroes), became institutionalized on their own and played an influential role on the periphery of the political system.[11]

If revisionism was a consensual goal in interwar Hungary, there was no similar consensus regarding its achievement, for the simple reason that the international distribution of power and influence was scarcely favorable to such an endeavor. With an army limited by the peace treaty to 35,000 men and with a shattered

10 Macartney, *October Fifteenth*, 1:5. Two general accounts of the Trianon era are Gusztáv Grátz, *A forradalmak kora: Magyarország története, 1918–1920* (Budapest, 1935), and Oscar Jászi, *Revolution and Counterrevolution in Hungary* (London, 1924).

11 Macartney, *October Fifteenth*, 1:28ff.

21

economy, revisionism at the start was little more than a passionate aspiration. This state of impotence fostered some integral revisionists, who viewed any mutilation of the realm of St. Stephen and any fragmentation of the Carpathian Basin's geographical and economic unity as an affront to reason and logic and Christian faith, but they found themselves increasingly a minority as the turbulence of the immediate postwar years gave way to a semblance of stability. A more moderate brand of irredentism, which emphasized the ethnic rather than the historical demerits of the Trianon treaty, and which made partial revision—hopefully by peaceful means—its objective, prevailed in official circles as well as with the majority of the population.

The counterrevolutionary conservatism that in varying degrees characterized pre-entry governments had historical roots in the aristocratic, paternalistic pattern of social and political relationships which replaced the more feudal practices after 1848. The experience with the Soviet Republic of 1919 served, however, to turn this conservatism from a class-based Weltanschauung into a more consensual phenomenon that was almost ideological in its rejection of any left-wing values and manifestations. All through the interwar period reform movements suffered from the precedent of the Kun regime's excesses, although it must be added that the mainstream of this counterrevolutionary conservatism proved equally inimical to the values and movements of the extreme right.[12] As will be seen, it was the identification of revisionist nationalism with the maintenance of the prevailing social order which

[12] An attempt to evaluate "alien" ideologies in a Hungarian context can be found in Gyula Szekfű, *Három Nemzedék,* 2d ed. (Budapest, 1934).

endowed the regency governments with their remarkable staying power.

Hungary's Western cultural orientation dates back to the early establishment of the Roman church and was scarcely affected by the long Turkish occupation, for the Turks were not given to proselytizing and left no mark on the intellectual and religious life of the country; Habsburg rule likewise did nothing to weaken this orientation. The national revival in the nineteenth century was more inward-looking than cosmopolitan and eventually brought about a reaction that was manifested in such activities as the founding of the review *Nyugat* [West] in 1908, which aimed to reinvigorate cultural contacts with Western ideas. The importance of literature as a vehicle of social comment for a small and linguistically isolated nation such as Hungary can hardly be overemphasized, and, as will be seen, this function prevailed even in the post-entry period. The rise of the populist movement in the twenties and thirties must therefore be viewed in this perspective. The populists represented a reaction to the conservatism that permeated the political culture; they were aroused specifically by the plight of the rural proletariat. United by this common concern, the populists—some of whom styled themselves as "village explorers"—set out to investigate the social problems of the poorer peasantry and to lift the latter out of their economic and cultural doldrums.[13] In the main they had left-wing political convictions, and ultimately the movement furnished, in men like Gyula Illyés, Ferenc Erdei, and József Darvas, the core of the literary and cultural establishment of the communist era. Popu-

---

[13] An account of the state of the peasantry is given in István Szabó, *A magyar parasztság története* (Budapest, 1940).

lism was divided by the question of priorities from the so-called urbanists, an equally reform-minded but more heterogeneous group which included the poet Attila József and which focused on the problems of the growing urban proletariat. Both populists and urbanists were predominantly national reformers, seeking indigenous solutions to indigenous exigencies, and owing little to the transnational ideologies of the day. The political activities of the "village explorers" were necessarily limited by the profound conservatism of the political establishment, and when in March, 1937, they made public a radical reform program their organization was dissolved.

Of the more extreme ideologies that existed in the political spectrum of the interwar period, Marxism-Leninism had not struck deep roots in Hungary, partly because it clashed with the Christian ethos and the dominant value of nationalism, and partly because of the Kun experience. Although agents of the Comintern operated in Hungary, and some cryptocommunists belonged to the Social Democratic Party, the mass of the people proved singularly unreceptive to this new religion. Ideologies of the extreme right, being inherently nationalistic, gained more adherents, but once again the end product proved to be characteristically indigenous. Apart from some popular sympathy for the corporatist experiment in Fascist Italy (prompted in part by Italian support for Hungarian revisionism), the chief manifestation of the extreme right could be found in the "Hungarist" movement initiated by Ferencz Szálasi.[14] The ideology of the movement, which was founded in 1936 and eventually became the Arrow Cross Party, consisted of nine parts nationalism and one part national socialism. Hitler's

[14] Macartney, *October Fifteenth,* 1:160ff.

low regard for the Magyars, although omitted from Hungarian editions of *Mein Kampf,* was scarcely calculated to gain their ideological allegiance, and even his closest counterpart in Hungary, Szálasi, stressed the goal of Magyar supremacy in the Carpathian Basin and was rather less concerned with the anti-Semitic and totalitarian aspects of the dogma. In any event "Hungarism" attracted marginal support, and least of all from the political establishment; its nationalism had no novelty value, while its social and economic aspects were secondary and ill-defined. Only the German occupation in 1944 would bring Szálasi and the Arrow Cross to momentary power.

To recapitulate, the predominant belief system was conservative but nonideological, culturally Western-oriented but politically at odds with the status quo powers. It viewed the Hungarian nation as the victim of a gross injustice and was thereby attuned to the other revisionist powers. Internally, it rejected outright the social revolutionary precedents of Dózsa and Kun and was in some respects more conservative than the political culture of the Kossuth era. The political élite embodied and propagated all of these values; right radicalism appealed most to the insecure elements of the middle class and to the military caste; left radicalism had support among the urban Jewish middle classes and among industrial workers, while its populist variant drew its strength from the disaffected sections of the peasantry.

Socioeconomic Patterns

Hungary's social structure in the pre-entry period can be dissected along several dimensions, with the variables combining to form various patterns of social behavior. One important cleavage that had been deepened by industrialization in the latter half of the nineteenth century was that dividing country from city. The interests of the urban working classes and of the bourgeoisie had become distinct and different from those of the rural landowners and of the peasantry. The cleavage between the capital and the provincial hinterland became most pronounced at the end of World War I, when the overwhelmingly urban Social Democrats and the workers' and soldiers' councils came to power in Budapest; while most of the bourgeoisie recoiled in horror, the strongest opposition came from the rural gentry and the peasantry, and when Admiral Horthy rode into the capital on his white horse, he castigated Budapest for being a "sinful city."[15] The ensuing reprisals—the so-called White Terror—directed at the radical leaders of the socialist proletariat were frenzied but short-lived.

A more enduring social legacy of the Soviet Republic was a widespread, if generally passive, anti-Semitism elicited by the fact that Kun and the majority of his lieutenants had been Jews and by the radicalism of much of the Jewish intelligentsia, who thereafter continued to play a prominent role in the Social Democratic Party as well as in the communications industry.[16] The over-all social distribution of the Jews also singled them out, this time not for their radicalism but for their preponderance in the commercial, financial, cultural, and educational spheres. It has been

[15] See István Deák, "Budapest and the Hungarian Revolutions of 1918–1919," *The Slavonic and East European Review,* 46, no. 106 (1968) : 129–40.

[16] R. V. Burks, *The Dynamics of Communism in Eastern Europe* (Princeton, 1961), p. 200; cf. George Gömöri, "Social Conflicts in Hungarian Literature, 1920–1965," *Journal of International Affairs,* 20, no. 1 (1966) : 152ff., and Gábor Radnai, *A zsidók az ellenforradalomban* (Budapest, 1920).

pointed out elsewhere that the social stratification of the Jews was the inverse of that of the Magyar population, for the proportion of the former among the peasantry, the industrial working classes, and in the military establishment and state administration was negligible, whereas their number in the professional and entrepreneurial occupations was disproportionately large.[17] Whatever the original incentives and discrimination that led to this asymmetry, the resultant anti-Semitism remained as a latent and disintegrative force.

Inflation and the economic collapse at the end of the Great War brought to the middle classes and to the gentry an economic insecurity that was only magnified by their political impotence in those unsettled years. When the Treaty of Trianon ended Hungarian administration of territories taken over by the successor states, the numbers of the middle classes were swollen by the influx of Magyar officials, who had up to then manned some 90 per cent of the administrative posts. This large group of refugees—irredentist, politically active, highly trained, and unemployed—formed almost a class of its own, and one that the postwar administrations had to reckon with. The insecurity of the middle classes did not bring them directly to political power, but it led to their implicit alliance with the ruling establishment of aristocrats and gentry. Under the latter's over-all administration, then, the bourgeoisie was firmly in control of the urban environment throughout the pre-entry period, the working classes being most quiescent under Bethlen; rural Hungary remained in the hands of the large landowners, with a self-satisfied class of peasant freeholders and a large but voiceless agrarian proletariat.[18]

[17] Macartney, *October Fifteenth*, 1:19–21.

[18] Estimates of the size of social classes are, in view of the difficulty of accurate identification and enumeration, seldom

This survey of the social structure would be incomplete without a brief note on the military subsystem, for the latter was to exert a strong influence on the secular decision-making apparatus of the state. The *kaiserlich und königlich* military establishment of the Dual Monarchy had been primarily an Austrian and German-speaking organization, and, although there existed a strictly Hungarian militia (the Honvéd), all the higher staff officers had to pass through the Austrian academies and staff colleges.[19] It was almost by a process of natural selection that a disproportionately high number of ethnically German ("Swabian") Hungarians gravitated to the *k. und k.* forces and there rose to staff level. When, in the peacetime Hungarian army, they eventually reached the highest posts, their background frequently manifested itself in a Germanophilism that led to disastrous disregard for political authority. A case in point was the behavior of the chief of the general staff appointed in 1938, General Werth, who consistently urged Hungary's participation in the German war effort and who on the occasion of the German occupation of Yugoslavia in 1941 took a posi-

---

incontrovertible, but one such profile of the prewar system allots 6 per cent to the upper class, 8 per cent to the middle class (including the semirural gentry), 37 per cent to the industrial working class and the petit bourgeoisie, and 49 per cent to the peasantry; see Károly Nagy, "The Impact of Communism in Hungary," *East Europe*, 18, no. 3 (1969) : 13. Strikes occurred more frequently in the thirties, the most notable being that of the Budapest construction workers in August, 1935. For the fluctuations in trade-union membership in the pre-entry period, see Helmreich, *Hungary*, p. 264. Cf. George G. Heltai, "Changes in the Social Structure of the East European Countries," *Journal of International Affairs*, 20, no. 1 (1966) : 166.

[19] See Macartney, *October Fifteenth*, 1 : 15–17, and Ithiel de Sola Pool, ed., *Satellite Generals* (Stanford, Calif., 1955), p. 96.

tion diametrically opposed to that of Prime Minister Teleki.[20]

The occupational profile of the population placed Hungary in a mixed industrial-agricultural category. In 1930 the following distribution prevailed:[21]

Agriculture, forestry, fisheries	51.8%
Extractive industries	1.3
Industry	21.7
Commerce and finance	5.4
Communications	3.9
Public services and professions	5.0
Others	10.9

The proportion engaged in agricultural occupations was smaller for Hungary than for all but one of the East European countries now in the communist system:[22]

Yugoslavia (1931)	76%
Bulgaria (1926)	75
Rumania (1930)	72
Poland (1931)	60
Czechoslovakia (1930)	33

An early attempt was made to reduce the number of landless laborers through the Land Reform Act of 1920, when about 13 per cent of the arable land was redistributed to benefit more than half a million persons. As a result, by 1930 landholders and their families accounted for 60.91 per cent, and day laborers and em-

[20] Macartney, *October Fifteenth,* 1:480ff.
[21] *Ibid.,* p. 64.
[22] Wilbert E. Moore, *Economic Demography of Eastern and Southern Europe* (Geneva, 1945), p. 26.

ployees for 39.09 per cent, of all agricultural workers. These figures, however, did not reflect the true state of Hungarian agriculture, for .004 per cent of landowners still controlled 43 per cent of the total land area, while at the other end of the scale dwarf holdings were also numerous; medium-sized holdings were fewer in Hungary than in the neighboring countries of Eastern Europe.[23] Emigration, a shift to other occupations, and further resettlement programs progressively reduced the number of landless peasants to the still-high figure of 746,000 in 1941.[24] Agricultural overpopulation remained particularly heavy in the Alföld and in the north.

Despite the polarization outlined above, Hungary's agricultural productivity grew throughout the preentry period; although it stood below the average for all of Europe, it was surpassed in Eastern Europe only by Czechoslovakia, and productivity in the Magyar-German areas of Rumania and Yugoslavia was higher than in the rest of the East European countries.[25] In the industrial and extractive sectors of her economy Hungary suffered from the loss of territories and internal markets, but discoveries of manganese, bauxite, and oil, and the development of new industries, such as textiles, contributed to a rise in production and employment.[26] Between 1920 and 1928 the index of in-

[23] Béla A. Balassa, *The Hungarian Experience in Economic Planning* (New Haven, Conn., 1959), p. 25. Some large estates were owned not by individuals but by corporations or the churches. Cf. A. Körmendy-Ekes, "Big Estates in Hungary," *Hungarian Quarterly,* 3 (Spring, 1937) : 43–58.

[24] Helmreich, *Hungary,* p. 232.

[25] Moore, *Economic Demography,* pp. 35, 38.

[26] See Helmreich, *Hungary,* pp. 291–92. Another factor retarding industrialization was the conservatism of the large landowners, who exerted a powerful influence on the governments of the interwar period.

dustrial production jumped from 100 to 294, and after a sharp drop in the depression period it continued to rise, particularly when wartime needs brought about a large increase in capacity. By 1941 one-quarter of the population was engaged in extractive and other industrial activities. Indeed, in the 1930's only Czechoslovakia had a higher per capita income than Hungary.[27]

The Political System

The anomie of the immediate postwar days was replaced by a period of reconstruction and internal integration in which the various governments' quest for legitimacy was facilitated by the revisionist-nationalist ethos. The generally apolitical style of administration which characterized these governments was a product as well as a cause of the prevailing low degree of social mobility and the limited political participation of the rural and urban proletariat.

The first postwar National Assembly, elected in 1920 by secret balloting on the basis of a wide franchise (with the abstention of the Social Democrats, still in official disgrace), re-established the old Constitution of the Kingdom of Hungary and named Admiral Horthy regent and acting head of state. When in 1921 Charles IV made two attempts to return to Hungary and claim the crown, the opposition of the antilegitimists (added to the not negligible pressure of the Western Powers) prevailed, and the Habsburg dynasty's ties with Hungary were definitively severed.

[27] Balassa, *The Hungarian Experience in Economic Planning*, p. 26; cf. Iván T. Berend and György Ránki, *Magyarország gazdasága az első világháboru után, 1919–1929* (Budapest, 1966).

31

That same year Count István Bethlen, a conservative Transylvanian aristocrat, was appointed prime minister, and during the ensuing decade his paternalistic but capable administration guided the country's fortunes. He was by no means a convinced democrat; the electoral reform of 1922 stipulated open voting in rural areas, and this, coupled with the fact that county officials were socially and ideologically indistinguishable from the political élite, militated against the effective political participation of the peasantry.

The 1922 general election set an enduring pattern.[28] The "Government Party," the Party of Unity, was a coalition of several groups, including the Smallholders, and obtained 143 of 245 seats; lacking any well-defined ideology, it served mainly to let the administration proceed unhampered by the vagaries of electoral politics. The Social Democratic Party, with a vaguely Marxist ideology, elected twenty-five deputies, but its wings were clipped by a previous formal agreement with Bethlen under which the Social Democrats would abstain from rural politics and undertake to keep the trade-unions out of the political sphere. Other main parties later included the National Liberals, whose liberal, middle-class, Jewish character destined them for near-extinction by the end of the thirties, the Independent Smallholders, a moderately progressive party with rural support, and the Peasant Union. The activities of these opposition parties (a truly "loyal" opposition!) seldom went beyond the registering of dissenting opinions. At the extremes of the political spectrum, neither communists nor nazis developed

[28] See Macartney, *October Fifteenth,* 1:49ff. Greater stress is placed on the resilience of left-wing movements in this period by Ilona Pándi, *Osztályok és pártok a Bethlen-konszolidáció időszakában* (Budapest, 1966).

very effective forms of participation. The former had been outlawed and their leaders lived in exile; Kun eventually lost his life in one of Stalin's purges. A few communist agents, notably Mátyás Rákosi, were dispatched by Moscow to foment the occasional strike and to infiltrate the trade-union movement and the Social Democratic Party, but few escaped arrest and in any event they faced a hostile environment. The main right-wing movement, the Arrow Cross, remained in the political wilderness until October, 1944.

This party system functioned reasonably well to articulate the various interests in the country, except those of the rural poor, whose fate became the special concern of the populists. However, the lack of a firm parliamentary tradition and the extraordinary economic and external problems besetting Hungary after the war left the parties as ineffectual observers of the actual administrative process, and neither of the two houses in Parliament played a major role in policy-making. The head of state, Admiral Horthy, was constitutionally commander-in-chief of the armed forces and had the right of suspensory veto over legislation and of choosing the head of government, subject to Parliament's approval; as it happened, he never exceeded his constitutional powers and scarcely fitted the image of a dictator which has been attributed to him by some chroniclers.[29] Effective power rested with the political élite of aristocrats and gentry and with the state bureaucracy.

Bethlen made no attempt to politicize the masses or to significantly alter the existing social and economic order. The recruitment function in his system was predetermined by the ascriptive nature of the political

---

[29] Macartney, *October Fifteenth,* 1:49ff.

élite as well as by the surplus of middle-class and gentry administrative talent. The system responded exceedingly well to the revisionist consensus; its regulative capability was also demonstrably high. Bethlen attempted to pacify the urban working class with a wide range of social legislative measures, enacted between 1921 and 1930, which regulated or prescribed pensions, social insurance, minimum age, and working conditions.[30]

The most urgent problem facing Bethlen's government was the state of the economy; inflation, lost industries and markets, reparations, and unemployment were all facets of this problem. Desperately short of capital, Bethlen pragmatically made peace with the successor states and in 1924 negotiated a loan that brought with it League of Nations supervision of Hungary's finances. This program of reconstruction eventually bore fruit, and by 1930 even a favorable balance of trade was achieved. The unemployment, most serious among middle-class professionals and administrators, was resolved by the expedient of enlarging the government bureaucracy; industrialization and a declining birth rate in rural areas combined to alleviate somewhat the hidden unemployment plaguing the agricultural labor force.

The Great Depression hit Hungary in 1930–31 with the collapse of the world-market price of wheat–her largest single export. Bethlen resigned in the face of peasant and middle-class antagonism, and subsequent regimes were saddled once again with the task of economic reconstruction. The ultimate success of that reconstruction was intimately tied to Hungary's evolving role on the international level and will therefore

[30] See Béla Kovrig, *Magyar táradalompolitika, 1920–1945* (New York, 1954).

be considered in that context. Bethlen's fall, however, had a further important consequence; it unleashed anti-Semitic and right-radical forces that he had successfully held in check for ten years.

Patterns of Integration

The Versailles peace treaties altered the map of central and eastern Europe, theoretically to make it congruent with the dictates of national self-determination, and established the League of Nations to enforce this new order. The execution of the first objective was flawed by pragmatic and essentially political considerations; the effectiveness of the League, on the other hand, was qualified from the start by discord among the Entente Powers and by America's return to isolationism. The resulting European international system was characterized by national particularism, by a cleavage between the defenders of the status quo and the revisionist powers, and by an institution for the resolution of conflicts whose success depended upon a hypothetical concert of the victorious powers.

In Eastern Europe the limited degree of regional integration achieved by the Dual Monarchy was erased and replaced by a new configuration of states which scarcely solved the economic and ethnic problems of the area; a more logical federative solution had been beyond the capacity of the peacemakers. Consequently, throughout the pre-entry period Eastern Europe was divided into two unequal camps—the successor states, which included Czechoslovakia, Rumania, and Yugoslavia, and the revisionist states, Hungary and Bulgaria. The former faced the difficult task of integrating often disparate elements into viable national societies and understandably advocated rigid adherence to the terms of the treaties to which they owed their existence. This existence was potentially threatened in turn by the equally nationalistic revisionism that predominated in Hungary. There was thus a basic incompatibility in the national goals of the two camps which relegated hopes of region-wide integration to the limbo of academic speculation. Instead, there evolved various alignments that served to deepen the existing cleavages.

It was within this unpromising conjuncture that the Bethlen regime set out to construct a new Hungarian foreign policy. Hungary's requests for plebiscites in the severed territories were refused (with the exception of Sopron, near the Austrian border, which voted to remain in Hungary), and there was no recourse but to accept the status quo. This acquiescence was prompted not only by legal treaty obligations but also by more pragmatic considerations. One of these was the marked military inferiority imposed by the peace treaty: an army of 35,000 men and production of small arms only.[31] These stipulations ruled out—at least in the twenties and early thirties—any military venture in quest of territorial revision. The pressing need for economic reconstruction also relegated revision to the status of a long-term aspiration. In 1922 Hungary had been admitted to the League of Nations, and the following year she asked for the Reparation Commission's sanction to suspend reparation payments so that she could float a loan on the international money market. The successor states voiced misgivings about the possible uses that such a loan would be put to by a revisionist Hungary, but following the latter's

[31] Macartney, *October Fifteenth,* 1:87.

guarantees that she would respect the stipulations of the Treaty of Trianon, two protocols were signed in March, 1924, which embodied these guarantees and a new schedule of reparation payments. Thereupon a loan of 250 million gold crowns was arranged, with the further proviso that Hungary's public finances be subject to League supervision; the successful outcome of these negotiations in turn facilitated the reconstruction program of the Bethlen government.

Over-all economic cooperation and integration in the Danubian Basin showed no progress in the period between the Great War and World War II. The economic unity and quasi-autarchy of the Dual Monarchy had been maintained by a wall of high tariffs, so that at the turn of the century fully three-quarters of Hungary's imports originated in the Austrian half of the empire. This imperfect and somewhat artificial common market was terminated by the territorial settlement of 1920, and in subsequent years the various new states sought to find their place in a less protective economic environment.[32] The resulting trade policies, imposing controls and tariffs that surpassed even the prewar pattern, were motivated by political considerations. Nonetheless, regional trade links did not vanish; just prior to the depression, Bulgaria, Czechoslovakia, Poland, and Rumania were responsible for more than a third of Hungary's imports and more than a quarter of her exports. But a reorientation of Hungary's trade toward countries that were politically more sympathetic was accelerated by the depression and by the renewed in-

[32] See John Michael Montias, "Economic Nationalism in Eastern Europe: Forty Years of Continuity and Change," in *Eastern Europe in Transition*, ed. Kurt London (Baltimore, 1966), pp. 173-203, and n.a., *Magyarország Külkereskedelme, 1919–1945* (Budapest, 1961).

terest of Germany and Italy in East European affairs. Moreover, the economic crash stimulated protective tendencies in the area; for instance, in 1930 Czechoslovakia terminated her trade agreement with Hungary, and for the next six years there prevailed between the two countries a tariff war during which trade was carried on mainly by barter deals. As Hungarian revisionism grew in intensity in the thirties, her trade with Rumania and Czechoslovakia fell to a fraction of its pre-depression volume and remained stagnant.[33] Austria, Germany, and Italy, on the other hand, became in that same period Hungary's best trade partners. Trade agreements with Austria in 1922 and 1926 had already cut import duties by 50 per cent on a number of specified products, and they were renewed in 1932 after a brief tariff skirmish. A 1931 trade agreement with Germany gave a 25 per cent tariff preference to Hungarian wheat. And the Hungarian-Italian Commercial and Navigation Treaty of 1928 provided, *inter alia,* for some tariff reductions.

Hungary's economic position in 1932 was, however, still determined by her wheat sales. The market of the successor states was rapidly disappearing, the preference agreement with Germany had applied only to 1931, and the Austrian market, though it continued to absorb some 30 per cent of Hungary's exports, had its own size limitations. Consequently, Hungary turned to her remaining sympathetic neighbor, Italy, with a proposal for closer Austro-Hungarian-Italian economic cooperation leading to an eventual customs union.[34] Germany approved of the idea, but France and the successor states saw in it a threat to the Cen-

[33] Montias, "Economic Nationalism in Eastern Europe," pp. 174–77.
[34] See Macartney, *October Fifteenth,* 1:96ff.

tral European status quo and accordingly put forward
the Tardieu Plan, which recommended the full economic integration of the Danubian states and, by im-
plication, recognition by the latter of the permanence
of the 1920 boundaries. Hungary and Rumania voiced
economic objections, and, in the event, lack of support
from Germany, Italy, and Britain killed the plan. The
Stresa Conference of 1932, having considered the problem of revitalizing the Danubian economies, agreed
that exchange and trade restrictions would have to be
lifted, but its recommendations proved equally futile.

Unlike these two plans, Hungary's initiatives in
Rome and Vienna prevailed, and on March 15, 1934,
the Rome Protocols were signed. The Protocols embodied preferential trade agreements that favored
Hungarian wheat and Austrian and Italian industrial
products and timber. Negotiations on a customs union
did not go further and, although a more secure market
for wheat was not a negligible gain for Hungary, the
ultimate importance of the Protocols lay less in the
commercial advantages than in the symbolic alignment
of the signatories.[35]

The extension of the German economic sphere in
the thirties resulted in a rapid increase in German-
Hungarian trade, and it was maintained at a high
level during the years of World War II by the requirements of the nazi military machine.[36] Germany's economic and industrial power was guided, of course, by
political considerations; thus, by 1938 German trade
with Hungary far surpassed predepression levels,
whereas the former's trade with Czechoslovakia fell

[35] For a comparison of Hungary's trade with Austria and
Italy before and after the Protocols, see *ibid.*, p. 145.

[36] See Antonin Basch, *The Danube Basin and the German
Economic Sphere* (New York, 1943).

39

by one-half in the same period.[37] The degree of economic integration on the eve of World War II is illustrated by the following indices:[38]

	Percentage Share in Hungarian	
	Imports (1938)	Exports
Austria	11.5	18.3
Bulgaria	0.8	1.0
Czechoslovakia	6.7	4.1
Germany	30.1	27.4
Great Britain	6.3	8.1
Italy	6.3	8.5
Poland	1.4	1.0
Rumania	9.8	4.0
Soviet Union	0.1	0.1
United States	5.3	2.4
Yugoslavia	4.5	3.0
Others	17.3	22.1

The Axis Powers (Germany, Austria, and Italy) accounted for roughly half of Hungary's trade; the other East European states (Bulgaria, Czechoslovakia, Poland, Rumania, and Yugoslavia) provided in the ag-

[37] Montias, "Economic Nationalism in Eastern Europe," p. 176.
[38] Központi Statisztikai Hivatal, *Magyar statisztikai zsebkönyv, 1968* (Budapest, 1968), pp. 96–97; hereinafter cited as *MSZ, 1968.*

gregate 23.2 per cent of Hungary's imports and took 13.1 per cent of her exports. The political realities of the era are clearly reflected in this polarized trade pattern.

Although economic considerations predominated in Hungary's foreign policy in the Bethlen period, her contemporary international outlook foreshadowed the alignments of the thirties.[39] Dissatisfaction with the peace settlement, at times covert, at others vociferous, dictated the search for friends in the international community. The main successor states—Czechoslovakia, Rumania, and Yugoslavia—were by definition ruled out, and all the more so when in 1921 they entered into a series of bilateral agreements, designed to contain Hungary, which were collectively known as the Little Entente. A few tentative discussions with Beneš over partial revision of the Czechoslovak-Hungarian boundary proved fruitless, and Bethlen's policy toward the successor states was one of reciprocated hostility manifested in attempts to arouse the Magyar and other minorities and to weaken the Entente's common resolve. Despite the loss of the Burgenland, relations with Austria showed steady improvement and were cultivated, but in the European power balance truncated Austria counted for little. Of the less proximate powers, France, while not unfriendly, became a staunch supporter of the Little Entente;[40] Britain, with the exception of the Rothermere press, did not support revision; the other potentially revisionist power, Germany, was preoccupied with internal prob-

[39] See Macartney, *October Fifteenth,* 1:81–88.
[40] Franco-Hungarian relations became strained for a while after the discovery of a bizarre plot (to which some of the political élite were privy) to support revisionist propaganda with forged French francs.

41

lems until the thirties; and the Soviet Union, which in any case was anathema to the Hungarians, had, like the United States, withdrawn into isolation.

The international environment was evidently not one that favored quick settlement of the territorial problems in Eastern Europe, and Bethlen consequently adopted a policy of gradualism as the minimum response to the consensual irredentism. At the League of Nations the Hungarian delegation, led initially by Count Albert Apponyi, kept up a barrage of protests at the mistreatment of Hungarian minorities in Slovakia, Yugoslavia, and particularly in Rumania.[41] Otherwise, Yugoslavia was considered the weakest link in the Little Entente, and Hungarian policy therefore strove both to stimulate Croatian separatism and to achieve a rapprochement with Belgrade; the latter tactic led in 1926 to a secret proposal for a nonagression treaty, but in that round the Little Entente's solidarity prevailed.[42] Bethlen was more successful in establishing the basis of Hungarian-Italian cooperation when in April, 1927, he signed a treaty of friendship with Mussolini. The latter's active interest in the Balkans prompted him to give verbal support to Hungarian revisionism and specifically to plot with Hungary for the dismemberment of Yugoslavia and the creation of an independent Croatian state. Although Bethlen at times repeated Kossuth's warning that a fragmented Eastern Europe could scarcely escape eventual German or Russian suzerainty, resolution of

[41] An authoritative analysis of the minorities problem in both Hungary and the successor states is given by G. C. Paikert, "Hungary's National Minority Policies, 1920–1945," *The American Slavic and East European Review*, 12, no. 2 (1953) : 201–18.

[42] Macartney, *October Fifteenth*, 1:84.

the prevailing cleavages seemed beyond the capacity of any of the actors concerned.[43]

For a year after Bethlen's resignation the government was headed by Count Gyula Károlyi, but the latter had to comply with the demands of Hungary's creditors for strict financial orthodoxy and was forced to resign by the same pressures that had ousted Bethlen. The new prime minister, who came to power in September, 1932, was General Gyula Gömbös, an anti-Semitic right radical and an advocate of close alignment with Italy and Germany. Gömbös was equally disliked by old-line conservatives and by the liberal and left-wing parties; the economic crisis, however, swelled the numbers of disaffected middle- and working-class people who were attracted by right radicalism and its assessment of the crisis in terms of the dominance of Jewish capital. Under Gömbös a *numerus clausus* law set a ceiling on Jewish membership in certain professions and in business; in other internal respects his regime followed the path of economic orthodoxy despite his dream of setting up a fascist state. Externally, the new prime minister's first act was to travel to Rome and engage in an orgy of mutual congratulations with Mussolini, who obliged his guests by declaring that the Treaty of Trianon had been "inspired by political calculations which time and experience had already condemned."[44] Hungary's close alignment with Italy was thus reaffirmed, much to the chagrin of those groups who still hoped that France might in time come around to seeing the justice of Hungary's demands. Hardly had Hitler consolidated

[43] See Count Stephen Bethlen, *The Treaty of Trianon and European Peace* (New York, 1934).
[44] Quoted in Macartney, *October Fifteenth,* 1:115.

his position in 1933 than Gömbös journeyed to Berlin, there to learn of Germany's plans for Eastern Europe. These were not entirely encouraging: Hungary could press her claims on Czechoslovakia once Germany had moved in that direction, but German interests precluded revision at the expense of Rumania or Yugoslavia. Germany's more favorable response to the economic needs of Hungary has already been noted.[45] Austria's future was also a matter of contention, and consequently the Rome Protocols of 1934 openly flouted Hitler's plans for an *Anschluss*.

Relations with the Little Entente suffered a further setback when a Croatian terrorist assassinated King Alexander of Yugoslavia (together with French Foreign Minister Barthou) in Marseilles; Hungary was blamed for having harbored some of these "Ustaši" nationalists on her territory.[46] The year 1934 also witnessed diverse negotiations aiming for a general European pact, for an Italian-French front against Germany, for a Danubian pact, all of which stopped short of agreement. The alignments that did prevail, such as the defense treaties linking France, Czechoslovakia, and the Soviet Union, did more to accentuate than to alleviate the existing cleavages, leaving Hungary with her Italian orientation and her increasingly stifling relationship with Germany. Hitler's policies of dividing the East Europeans and bringing them into a German sphere of influence were eminently successful; political and economic enticements worked with Hungary, Rumania, Bulgaria, and Yugoslavia, and thereafter indigenous attempts at regional

[45] *Ibid.*, p. 138.
[46] For the account of Hungary's chief delegate to the League of Nations, see Tibor Eckhardt, *Regicide at Marseille* (New York, 1964).

integration—such as the Hodža "Danubian Plan" of 1937—were doomed to failure.[47]

Gömbös' rule had precipitated a certain political realignment in Hungary which opposed his right-radical supporters to a heterogeneous group—ranging from legitimists to Social Democrats—united by its apprehension that internally and externally Gömbös was taking Hungary down a perilous path. The prime minister's death in October, 1935, provided Horthy with the opportunity to appoint a more moderate man, Kálmán Darányi. The latter's efforts to contain the right radicals were short-lived, and in May, 1938, a Western-oriented financial expert, Béla Imrédy, succeeded him. Imrédy's strategy was a fine balancing act that foreshadowed much of Hungary's wartime foreign policy. Convinced—as were Horthy and much of the body politic apart from the right radicals—that the Western Powers would prevail in the coming confrontation, he strove to prevent Hungary's complete integration into the Axis bloc and to gain Western support for his policy of partial revision. The Hungarian leaders rejected German proposals that Hungary participate in military operations against Czechoslovakia, although by this time the General Staff had convinced itself of the invincibility of the *Wehrmacht* and a rearmament program was in full swing. But while at Munich Chamberlain acceded to German demands backed by German power, he felt

---

[47] The Bled Agreement of August 23, 1938, between Hungary and the Little Entente powers linked nonaggression with the resolution of the minorities problem; German opposition and Munich quickly nullified this tentative disposition to compromise. See Macartney, *October Fifteenth*, 1 : 237ff.; cf. Milan Hodža, *Federation in Central Europe: Reflections and Reminiscences* (London, 1942), and Magda Adám, *Magyarország és a kisantant a harmincas években* (Budapest, 1968).

no such compulsion with respect to Hungary's formal request that the ethnically Magyar areas of Slovakia be ceded back; this impasse proved to be of capital importance, for it strengthened the hand of those elements which had preached all along that Hungary's fortunes lay with the Axis Powers. Germany and Italy agreed to arbitrate the issue, with Ribbentrop opposing and Ciano defending Hungarian claims, and by the Vienna Award of November, 1938, a predominantly Magyar-inhabited strip was returned to Hungary. The British goverment at first sanctioned the award, then repudiated it two years later on somewhat specious grounds.[48]

By the first Vienna Award, however, the die had been cast, and Hungary became increasingly committed to the Axis. Early in 1939 she signed the Anti-Comintern Pact, left the League of Nations, and occupied the northeastern territory of Ruthenia. Concurrently, Imrédy had been replaced by Pál Teleki, an immensely popular scholar and politician, who persisted with the ill-fated balancing act. Negative factors included the growing electoral strength of the Arrow Cross Party and of right radicalism in general, the Germanophile urgings of the General Staff, and the strong German orientation of the Rumanian and Yugoslav regimes. Hungary avoided any involvement with the Polish campaign and made a final effort to effect a realignment toward the south by signing the internally popular Pact of Eternal Friendship with Yugoslavia in December, 1940. Earlier that year, however, another round of arbitration had resulted in the return of part of Transylvania to Hungary

[48] Macartney, *October Fifteenth*, 1 : 303; cf. John F. Montgomery, *Hungary: The Unwilling Satellite* (New York, 1947), pp. 20, 116.

through the second Vienna Award; as a *quid pro quo* Hungary agreed to adhere to the German-Italian-Japanese Tripartite Pact. Thus eternal friendship with Yugoslavia proved to be of short duration, for a *coup d'état* overthrew the Belgrade regime and brought about a German occupation. Unlike his military advisers, Teleki was adamant that German troops not cross Hungarian soil to effect the occupation. Feeling powerless to prevent this, he committed suicide, an act which, as Churchill observed, absolved his name before history, but could not extricate his country from the grasp of the Axis.[49] When Croatia declared itself independent, the last of this series of territorial revisions took place with the occupation of the Bácska (Voivodina). In June, 1941, following a mysterious air bombardment of the city of Kassa, Hungary became an active belligerent against the Soviet Union.

For much of the remainder of World War II, Hungary pursued a policy calculated to achieve the minimum military involvement that was compatible with the maintenance of the internal status quo and national sovereignty. The main protractors of this policy were the regent himself and such men as Miklós Kállay, prime minister from 1942 to 1944, and Ferenc Keresztes-Fischer, the minister of the interior. Thus, unlike the pattern in the other East European countries, Hungary's opposition to Germany came from

[49] Winston S. Churchill, *The Grand Alliance* (Boston, 1950), p. 168; cf. Gyula Juhász, *A Teleki-kormány külpolitikája, 1939–1941* (Budapest, 1964). A selection of documents bearing on Hungary's role in the war has been edited by Magda Adám *et al.*, *Magyarország és a második világháboru*, 3d ed. (Budapest, 1966). This work, in keeping with the contemporary bias of Hungarian historiography, lays great stress on the mistakes and follies of the various governments in the Horthy era.

within the ruling élite rather than from an underground movement. Internally, this resistance was not
unsuccessful: after the fall of Czechoslovakia, Hungary
retained the most democratic political system in the
Danubian region, one which nurtured opposition
parties and afforded a rare haven for indigenous and
other European Jews. There even arose a so-called
Independence Front, composed of Smallholders, Social
Democrats, National Peasants, and other progressives,
which planned overtly for eventual reforms.[50] Externally, Kállay's balancing act consisted of various
attempts to secure a separate peace with the Western
Allies while maintaining token military participation
on the Eastern front.[51] The lack of American concern
with the political aspects of a postwar settlement, the
shelving of British proposals for a Balkan invasion,
and the famous percentage agreement reached by
Churchill and Stalin in October, 1944, giving the

[50] The curious career of the eventual leader of this Front, the
Smallholder Endre Bajcsy-Zsilinszky, is sketched in a brief
biography by Lázló Dernői Kocsis, *Bajcsy-Zsilinzky* (Budapest,
1966). Zsilinszky's obsessive and romantic patriotism took him
from the extreme right in 1920 to a tenuous alliance with the
communists in 1944 and ultimately to execution (and a post-
humous place in the pantheon of communist heroes) on the
order of the Szálasi regime.

[51] For details of these attempts, see Nicholas Kállay, *Hungarian Premier* (London, 1954), pp. 360-87 and *passim; idem,*
"Come Over," *Hungarian Quarterly* (New York), April-June,
1962, p. 6; n.a., *The Confidential Papers of Admiral Horthy*
(Budapest, 1965), pp. 248–70; Sir Llewellyn Woodward, *British
Foreign Policy in the Second World War* (London, 1957), p.
480; Macartney, *October Fifteenth,* 2 : 161ff., 191ff., 204ff. See
also J. Pelényi, "The Secret Plan for a Hungarian Government
in the West at the Outbreak of World War II," *Journal of
Modern History,* 36 (1964) : 170–78. A recent monograph by
Nándor A. F. Dreisziger, *Hungary's Way to World War II*
(Toronto, 1968), provides a brief but thorough account of
Hungarian foreign policy in the immediate prewar period.

Soviet Union predominant influence in Hungary, were among the many factors that prevented Hungary from opting out.[52]

In 1944 Hitler's impatience with Hungarian procrastination brought about a greater military effort (although the ill-equipped army had suffered a disastrous defeat at Voronezh in January, 1943) under the pro-German prime minister Döme Sztójay. Jewish deportations, the obvious unfeasibility of a separate peace with the Western Allies, and the advance of the Red Army across the Carpathians prompted Horthy to make a belated attempt to withdraw from the war. On October 15, 1944, with his envoys already in Moscow, he announced Hungary's intention to surrender.[53] The Germans thereupon imprisoned Horthy, occupied the country, and installed Szálasi as their puppet.

For Hungary, as for the other East European countries, integration in the pre-entry period had meant partial or full incorporation into the German sphere of influence. Profound incompatibilities had prevented effective cooperation in the Danubian Basin, and without such cooperation the fragments of the Dual Monarchy were powerless to oppose the proximate big powers—first Germany, then, as will be seen, the Soviet Union. Moreover, support for economic and

[52] On the percentage deal, see Winston S. Churchill, *Triumph and Tragedy* (Boston, 1953), pp. 227–28; the debate over the advisability of opening up a Balkan front is summed up in Michael Howard, *The Mediterranean Strategy in the Second World War* (London, 1968), while American policies regarding the postwar settlement are succinctly analyzed in Arthur Schlesinger, Jr., "Origins of the Cold War," *Foreign Affairs*, 46, no. 1 (1967) : 22–52.

[53] For the text of the proclamation, see Nicholas Horthy, *Memoirs* (London, 1956), pp. 323–25.

political integration into the Axis sphere existed among both the Hungarian élites and the masses. On the positive side, integration had facilitated postdepression reconstruction and had brought about partial revision of the Trianon boundaries; however, this had been achieved at the cost of much of Hungary's freedom of action and had placed her in the enemy camp with respect to the Western powers and the Soviet Union. The nature of the dilemma was seen clearly enough by the leadership and by the politically aware, but the motivating force of irredentism prevailed over other considerations. The process of integration was most pronounced in the military sphere, where the German and Hungarian General Staffs engaged in close collaboration; direction of the Hungarian economy, and of internal affairs in general, was not integrated, despite German attempts to impose system-wide procedures and coordination, until the occupation in 1944. Whatever internal consensus had existed in favor of collaboration with Germany at the time of the Vienna Awards (and indeed Italy, not Germany, had been recognized as the sympathetic arbiter), it dissipated rapidly with the progress of the war. When, toward the end of that conflict, the noted historian Gyula Szekfű wrote that somewhere Hungary had chosen the wrong road, he probably echoed the confusion and apprehensions of most Hungarians. How rewarding alternate roads might have been is idle speculation, for no country in Eastern Europe could have escaped the powerful influence of Germany and the Soviet Union.

3: INCORPORATION AND CONSOLIDATION, 1945–53

For the second time in less than thirty years, Hungary emerged from a world war on the losers' side, with her territory truncated and occupied and her social, political, and economic systems in a state of disarray. Symbolic of the political disintegration were the two governments that for a time existed concurrently, the puppets of two great armies. The quisling regime of Ferenc Szálasi was entirely dependent upon the Germans, his indigenous support being limited to the radical right; soon after siege was laid to Budapest by the Red Army on Christmas Day, 1944, his government moved to Sopron, where its expiry the following April coincided with the end of German resistance in Hungary. The other regime was a provisional administration, set up at Debrecen under Soviet auspices, which succeeded in fathering a government with genuine claims to democratic legitimacy. The subsequent incorporation into the Soviet system and the procrustean attempts to fit Hungary into a Stalinist mold followed a pattern that was broadly similar throughout Eastern Europe.[1] This chapter will consider the salient aspects of the Soviet-imposed

[1] For general acounts of the area-wide process of incorporation, see Hugh Seton-Watson, *The East European Revolution,* 3d ed. (New York, 1956), and H. Gordon Skilling, *The Governments of Communist East Europe* (New York, 1966).

process of integration, with a particular focus on those factors which are seen as relevant to the more secular trends toward (or away from) an East European community.

Territorial and Demographic Changes

Physical losses in territory and population came about as a direct or indirect result of Hungary's role in World War II. The territorial gains that had been achieved through the Vienna Awards or by outright annexation were nullified by the peace treaty, which even reduced the Trianon area by ceding a bridgehead of three villages across the Danube from Bratislava to Czechoslovakia. Since that time there has been no change in the territorial configuration of Hungary: the total area is 35,919 square miles (93,030 square kilometers), with 446 miles of common boundary with Czechoslovakia, 66 miles with the Soviet Union, 268 miles with Rumania, 397 miles with Yugoslavia, and 228 miles with Austria. Thus, in spite of her reduced size, Hungary remained astride the West's fluvial and main rail links with the Balkans. The postwar program of industrialization and industrial decentralization, however, altered the physiognomy of the various regions to some extent. In the Great Plains, cities such as Debrecen and Szeged grew in size and importance with the development or expansion of the ball-bearing, pharmaceutical, textile, and food industries; in the northern uplands, extractive and heavy industries led to rapid urbanization, particularly in the Miskolc area; similar developments occurred around Pécs in Transdanubia, while in the northeastern Little Plain Győr benefited from diverse industries.

Industrialization had numerous social and economic consequences, but for the moment we note that it altered the predominantly rural character of prewar Hungary.[2] Between 1949 and 1953 the urban population increased by 605,000 while the rural population suffered an absolute drop of 218,000: Greater Budapest numbered 1,728,000 persons in 1953, or about 19 per cent of the total population. Over-all demographic patterns were influenced by the war as well as by political decisions. The birth rate per thousand had dropped from a high of 29.4 in the early 1920's to 20.1 in the late 1930's, and the slower concurrent decline in the death rate contributed to the rather low rate of natural increase in the immediate prewar years. The phenomenon of natural regeneration, which frequently manifests itself in recently depopulated collectivities, brought the birth rate up to 20.4 per thousand and the natural rate of increase to 7.9 per thousand in the years 1946–50. Labor shortages and consequent difficulties with the first Five-Year Plan led in 1953 to a series of government decrees which aimed to boost the birth rate by banning abortions and limiting the sale of contraceptives. The policy may have been instrumental in bringing the rate of natural increase to its postwar peak of 12.0 per thousand in 1954, but the trend then reversed itself and the birth rate suffered a sustained decline.

Wartime losses, deportations, population exchanges, and emigration all had demographic consequences.[3] Military casualties numbered some 200,000 (140,000 from the Trianon territory), while an estimated half-million Jews (of whom 220,000 originated within the Trianon boundaries) lost their lives locally or in German concentration camps. Emigrants following the war included about 200,000 ethnic Germans who were

[2] Detailed statistics are given in Helmreich, *Hungary*, pp. 45–71.

[3] *Ibid.*, pp. 48–50.

expelled in accordance with the Potsdam Agreement,[4] a number of Jews heading for Israel, and anticommunist Hungarians whose exodus, however, was severely restricted by the border closure in 1948. The Czechoslovak-Hungarian transfer agreement of 1946 led to the emigration of 63,000 Slovaks and the inflow of 92,000 Magyars, the latter joining approximately 200,000 refugees from Transylvania, Slovakia, Ruthenia, and Voivodina. From the ethnic point of view these changes produced an even more homogeneous society; the remaining non-Magyar minorities made up no more than 4 per cent of the population, with the Germans still representing the largest ethnic component. The aggregate result of all these factors was, according to the census of 1949, a total population of 9,204,799; this figure actually represents a drop of 111,275 from the 1941 total for the same territory.[5] War casualties and the declining death rate also contributed to the relative aging of Hungarian society. In 1949 11.6 per cent of the population was sixty years of age or older; the proportion has been increasing steadily ever since (to 16.1 in 1967) and represents a continuing financial burden for the state. Educational reforms in the period of intensive socialization achieved a reduction in illiteracy to negligible levels. As for the distribution of population by religion, the 1949 census did not update the prewar data, from which indeed one could safely extrapolate, taking into account the decrease in the proportion of Jews; although religious practice was strongly discouraged after 1949, when the regime embarked on a secularizing campaign, the Roman Catholic church continued

---

[4] See Stephen Kertész, "The Expulsion of the Germans from Hungary: A Study in Postwar Diplomacy," *Review of Politics*, 15 (1953) : 179–208.

[5] *MSZ, 1968,* p. 11.

to claim some two-thirds of the population, with most of the remainder presumably finding their spiritual home in one or the other of the Protestant churches.[6]

Belief Patterns and the Social Structure

We have already seen how in the pre-entry period the political élite, in close alliance with the middle classes, fought a rear-guard action in defense of a paternalistic-authoritarian system, and how the issue of revisionism was used to rally the support of the peasantry and of the urban proletariat. When military defeat and German and Soviet occupation brought about the collapse of that political system, it became inevitable that its mainstays—the gentry and the aristocracy—would be eclipsed in their traditional political roles by new social forces. The old élites had been in the main antinazi as well as anticommunist, and consequently they bore the brunt of both German and Soviet purges; executions, deportations, and emigration virtually eliminated these classes from the Hungarian social structure. While it had marginal disintegrative consequences, their departure did not leave an ideological vacuum which could be easily filled by new revolutionary values. One of the briefing papers prepared for President Roosevelt prior to his journey to Yalta advised him that "the general mood of the people of Europe is to the left and strongly in favor of far-reaching economic and social reforms, but not, however, in favor of a leftwing totalitarian régime to achieve these reforms."[7]

[6] Helmreich, *Hungary,* pp. 65–67.
[7] U.S., Department of State, *The Conferences at Malta and Yalta* (Washington, D.C., 1955) , p. 103.

This assessment of the mood of Europe was applicable to Hungary, where the desire for reform was best articulated by the various political movements that had combined to form the "Independence Front." However, neither the latter nor the underground communists succeeded in developing an integrative myth of wartime resistance (which proved so effective in Yugoslavia, for instance), for reasons noted in the previous chapter; they could not overcome the nationalistic fervor of the pre-entry period which had driven them to the periphery of the political system. Thus, when after the war they stepped into the shoes of the old establishment, their claim to legitimacy was on the one hand strengthened by their long-standing commitment to social and economic reforms while on the other hand handicapped by the somewhat passive role they had played in prewar revisionism.

In the value system that prevailed after 1945, the old priorities were necessarily reversed: internal reform took primacy over any concern for territorial revision. As will be seen when we discuss the new political system, this reversal had a consensual basis which was evident particularly in the popularity of the 1945 land reform. Many of the factors, however, which after World War I had militated against any popularization of Marxist values were still in evidence. Identification of communism with the Soviet Union and of the latter with Pan-Slavism and the designs of the successor states was profoundly rooted in the national consciousness, and consequently, even after 1945, Hungary's political and cultural ethos was probably less receptive to the values that Stalin intended to implant in his newly acquired buffer zone than were the other East European countries. Reconstruction and modernization were general goals that found few opponents, and it was recognized that the country's prewar regimes had not been sufficiently active in this sphere; their implementation nevertheless remained qualified by nationalism, by a popular predilection for cultural links exclusively with the West, and by a Roman Catholic church which in Hungary had always been attuned to the values of the upper classes and to patriotism and which now maintained its adamant opposition to secular revolutionary movements.

As long as the prewar opposition parties and the indigenous progressive intelligentsia managed to hang onto the reins of power between 1945 and 1947, a tenuous state of compatibility prevailed between the belief system shared by most socioeconomic groups and the goals of the new noncommunist political élite; this was made clear enough by the voting patterns outlined below. However, the gradual acquisition of control by the communists brought to light a profound cleavage which produced the effective political alienation of the overwhelming majority of the population. The hard core of the Hungarian Communist Party numbered only a few thousand in 1945, and was composed of returning "Muscovite" exiles such as Mátyás Rákosi, Ernő Gerő, Mihály Farkas, József Révai, Gábor Péter, and Imre Nagy, and of "indigenous" communists like László Rajk and János Kádár, who had operated underground in Hungary; the majority had working-class origins and were Jews.[8] In the next few years the nucleus of the party gained adherents from the rural

[8] Biographical sketches of thirty-one contemporary leading figures of the Hungarian Workers' Party show that nineteen had a working-class or peasant background while eight came from the middle or lower-middle class, the social origins of the remaining four being indistinct. Helmreich, *Hungary,* pp. 392–409; cf. Burks, *Dynamics of Communism in Eastern Europe,* pp. 165–67.

and urban proletariat, from members of the defunct, extreme-right Arrow Cross Party, and from other sources, reaching a total of perhaps 200,000. According to 1947 estimates, the social composition of the party membership was 56 per cent workers, 37.3 per cent peasants, and 6.7 per cent middle class; the proportion of middle-class members was by far the lowest in Eastern Europe.[9] Electoral voting patterns did not, however, indicate a genuine class cleavage or a class-based clientele for the party, opposition being on the contrary diffused throughout the socioeconomic spectrum. This wide diffusion of anticommunist values was at the root of the "internal emigration" of the populace following Rákosi's seizure of power.

Sociological studies in other countries have shown that the peasantry is a repository of conservative values, and this was the case in Hungary, but with the important qualification that the key smallholder and kulak classes were unusually small. The political values of the large class of landless laborers were potentially radical, and indeed in the 1930's the "village explorers" had engaged in a campaign of politicization. Since Imre Nagy had been minister of agriculture in the provisional government when the 1945 land reform was promulgated, the Communist Party had every expectation of capitalizing on its role as the liberator of the rural poor to gain electoral support. It must have come as a shock, therefore, when the majority of the now landed peasantry asserted itself in favor of the status quo and against more radical Marxist reform; the eventual drive for collectivization only further alienated the rural classes.

In urban areas, on the other hand, the function of

[9] Burks, *Dynamics of Communism in Eastern Europe,* pp. 52–53.

mobilizing the industrial working classes had long been pre-empted by the Social Democratic Party and by the trade-unions, whose membership barely rose above 100,000 in the interwar period but which nonetheless had become well established in Hungary.[10] Although numerous new trade-unions were created after 1945, the working classes' traditional support of the Social Democrats suffered relatively little erosion in favor of the communists. This became evident when municipal elections were held in Budapest in October, 1945, for even a combined socialist-communist ticket failed to gain the expected absolute majority;[11] in the subsequent two general elections the Social Democrats insisted on running their own candidates. Thus, in the relatively democratic interregnum between 1945 and 1947, all the indicators pointed away from popular acceptance of Marxist values.

The incompatibility between basic consensual values and those of the communist élite necessitated draconian measures when the period of intensive socialist development began in 1948. The implantation of Marxist-Leninist ideology transformed the cultural and religious ethos as well as the social structure of the country. The party, having posited a rather spurious identity between its ideology and the interests of the "working classes," proceeded to ensure the unquestioned monopoly of these values in all spheres. Bour-

[10] By January 1947, trade-union membership had risen to 1,288,095. Helmreich, *Hungary*, p. 264; cf. Robert Gábor, *The Bolshevization of the Hungarian Trade Unions* (New York, 1952).

[11] The Smallholder Party gained 50 per cent of the vote, with the combined Socialist-Communist ticket taking 43 per cent and the remainder being divided among the Civic Democratic, National Peasant, and Hungarian Radical parties. Stephen D. Kertész, "The Methods of Communist Conquest: Hungary, 1944–47," *World Politics*, 3 (1950) : 40.

geois literary tendencies had to be eliminated, and, although some attempt was made to claim the parentage of the old progressive writers, the new Writers' Union became a mobilizing agent and appendage of the party. The minister of culture and chief ideologue, József Révai, told a congress of Hungarian writers in 1951 that literature was simply a weapon to defend the working classes and the "peace camp" and that socialist realism and dialectical materialism had to go hand in hand in this battle.[12] Literary creativity suffered a hiatus that was only emphasized by a concurrent campaign for cultural Russification in which the Soviet model was held to be the ultimate paradigm. This was most evident in the publishing field; until 1947 Hungarian and Western authors had predominated and the Russian contribution had been negligible, but by 1952 162 out of 277 "important publications" were translations of Soviet works.[13] It is scarcely surprising that the eventual de-Stalinization was ushered in by a restless literary establishment.

After the noncommunist political parties had disappeared the churches remained as the last focal point of ideological resistance, and the prince primate of the Roman Catholic church in Hungary, Cardinal Mindszenty, was particularly active in rallying these forces. The various churches had traditionally played a leading role in the educational system, a role which inevi-

[12] József Révai, "The Tasks of Hungarian Literature," *Társadalmi Szemle*, 6, no. 5 (1951) : 345–59. (The titles of articles in Hungarian periodicals will be cited in English.) Cf. József Révai, *Marxizmus, népiesség, magyarság* (Budapest, 1948) and Géza Hegedüs, *A polgári irodalom stilusirányai* (Budapest, 1947) .

[13] Another Russifying agent was the Hungarian-Soviet Society, a mass organization devoted to cultural, linguistic, and ideological penetration. Helmreich, *Hungary*, pp. 175, 180; cf. István Csicsery-Rónay, *Russian Cultural Penetration in Hungary*, 3d ed. (New York, 1952) .

tably came into conflict with the new directives for political indoctrination; accordingly, church schools were nationalized, while the cardinal was tried for conspiracy and imprisoned in February, 1949.[14] The State Office for Ecclesiastical Affairs thereupon acquired complete control over all religious matters. Hundreds of priests were banned, a corps of politically reliable "peace priests" was created, and subsidies to churches were projected to decrease to zero over a period of years; religious instruction in state schools was made optional and politically inadvisable, and by 1954 there remained only eight Catholic schools out of 3,148, four Calvinist schools out of 1,057, and one Lutheran school out of the 359 before the purge.

The military subsystem underwent a process of purification similar to that applied to all aspects of state administration, a process which aimed at the eradication of autonomous élites in Hungarian society. At the end of the war the communists, with the help of the Soviet military command, began the "de-nazification" of the army by introducing political advisers and by carefully vetting the officer corps. The political division of the Ministry of Defense, headed by General Pállfy-Oesterreicher, aimed to eliminate not so much those officers who had had pro-nazi leanings as those, mostly of upper-class origins, who had been the most loyal to Horthy and the most active in various armistice negotiations.[15] Pállfy himself lost his life in the Rajk purge

14 See Stephen Kertész, "Church and State in Hungary: The Background of the Cardinal Mindszenty Trial," *Review of Politics*, 11 (1949) : 208–19; cf. *The Trial of Josef Mindszenty* (Budapest, 1949), *Authorized White Book: Cardinal Mindszenty Speaks* (New York, 1949), and William Juhász, *Persecution of Churches Behind the Iron Curtain* (New York, 1952).

15 For the contemporary prime minister's account of Pálffy's activities and of Soviet pressures, see Ferenc Nagy, *The Struggle Behind the Iron Curtain* (New York, 1948), pp. 311ff.

of 1949, by which time only the most incompatible officers had been purged; by January, 1951, however, fully 80.7 per cent of the officer corps was newly appointed and came from politically desirable backgrounds.[16] The criterion of professional competence received short shrift in the period of reorganization, but the political reliability of the military élite was no longer in question.

All the measures outlined above served to overturn the old patterns of social stratification. The remnants of the upper classes and the administrative and professional middle classes became atomized and—at least physically—diffused throughout the new "classless" society. This was, of course, a consequence of official policy, and by the same token subsequent breakdowns according to class were largely speculative or ideologically motivated. The Communist Party's ideological monthly in 1951 published such a breakdown:[17]

		1930	1949
1.	Wage-earners		
	Workers	23.5%	27.7%
	White-collar	5.7	6.9
	Agricultural laborers	19.3	6.5
	Dwarf landholders	4.0	1.8
	Domestic help	2.3	1.1
	Pensioners	3.5	4.7
	Total	58.3	48.7
2.	Small farmers and craftsmen	28.7	43.3
3.	Landowners, capitalists, kulaks, merchants	10.9	6.9
4.	Professionals, etc.	2.1	1.1

[16] Pool, *Satellite Generals*, pp. 120ff.; cf. Helmreich, *Hungary*, pp. 144–50.

[17] "The Social Structure of Hungarian Society on the Basis of the 1949 Census," *Társadalmi Szemle*, 6, no. 6 (1951) : 491–97.

These statistics reflected the rise of the small land-holder class as a result of the 1945 land reform and the elimination of all "capitalists," the postwar figure for (3) comprising mainly the kulaks. The concurrent campaign for collectivization and industrialization gradually increased the proportion of the population in the wage-earner category. As will be seen, these attempts to eradicate class or religious identity and to impose a new, dogmatic belief system resulted in mass alienation rather than in the consolidation of the regime's internal legitimacy.

Patterns of Political and Economic Socialization

The long-illegal Communist Party returned to active politics in 1944 with the advance of the Red Army, and in December of that year it joined, under the sponsorship of the Soviet High Command, a motley group of opposition politicians to fill the vacuum left by the collapse of the old order. The Provisional National Assembly that met in Debrecen on December 21, 1944, had only 72 communists out of a total of 230 deputies and included representatives of the Smallholder, Social Democratic, and National Peasant parties.[18] The actual government also had a remarkably democratic appearance; it was headed by General Béla Miklós, who had gone over to the Russians following Horthy's armistice

[18] The Independent Smallholder Party had been founded in 1930 to replace its predecessor, which had joined the Bethlen coalition; the National Peasant Party, founded by the writer Imre Kovács, included many of the populists. The attempts of the old opposition parties to organize antinazi resistance and to coordinate their activities with the renascent communists are described in Macartney, *October Fifteenth,* vol. 2, chap. 19, and from a communist point of view by Gyula Kállai, *A magyar függetlenségi mozgalom* (Budapest, 1949).

proclamation, and included only three communist ministers. The Assembly agreed to seek an armistice and to effect a number of reforms that added up to the establishment of a pluralistic democratic system,[19] but the effectiveness of the provisional government was severely limited by the chaotic state of communications and by the power of ultimate sanction vested in the Soviet command.

There was much subsequent speculation as to why the Soviet Union did not immediately set up a "dictatorship of the proletariat" in Hungary. A certain deference to the sensibilities of the Western Allies may have been a contributing factor; furthermore, the returning Muscovites were acutely aware of their limited popularity and of the need for time to train cadres and to gain the favor of the least inimical social groupings. They set out to mobilize support through numerous new, officially apolitical functional organizations—youth groups, trade-unions, and the like—and to weaken the established political parties from within; in the accomplishment of these tasks the moral and logistical support of the High Command (and subsequently of the Soviet-dominated Allied Control Commission) proved invaluable. Initially, a guarded optimism prevailed, at least within the new noncommunist political élite, which was bolstered by the apparent acquiescence of communists and Russians in a democratic political system and by a literal reading of the Yalta Declaration

[19] The provisional government undertook to conclude an armistice with the Allies, to pay the reparations, to wage war against Germany, to repeal anti-Semitic and antidemocratic laws, to guarantee democratic rights and to institute universal and secret suffrage, to disband right-wing political movements and punish war criminals, and to effect a land reform. Macartney, *October Fifteenth*, 2:464.

on Liberated Europe, which guaranteed broadly representative governments in the liberated countries.[20]

The elections made it clear, however, that the Communist Party stood no chance of gaining power by democratic means, an outcome which Stalin at least seems to have anticipated.[21] These elections had a quality that was unique in Soviet-occupied Europe: in spite of many abuses and disfranchisements on assorted political grounds, they were relatively free and run by secret ballot. As was noted earlier, the communist tactic of holding preliminary municipal elections in Budapest, based on the assumption that the urban working classes would rally to the party, failed to achieve a plurality of the votes. In the November general elections, despite their material assets and the popularity of Imre Nagy's land reform, the communists fared even worse, gaining only 16.9 per cent of the votes and 70 out of 409 seats in Parliament. The Smallholders emerged as the strongest party, with 245 seats and 56.8 per cent of the popular vote, and the Social Democrats and National Peasants also made strong showings. Prior agreement of all the parties had been secured to maintain the coalition regardless of the outcome of the elections, and in the new cabinet the communists, supported by Marshal Voroshilov, insisted on holding the key portfolio of the interior. Having gained control of the state security apparatus and of the trade-unions, they proceeded systematically to undermine the position of the Smallholders, who were now characterized as the agents of reaction.

[20] For the text of the declaration, see World Peace Foundation, *Documents on American Foreign Relations, 1944–1945* (Washington, D.C., 1947), pp. 352–53.

[21] See Philip E. Mosely, *Face to Face with Russia* (Washington, D.C., 1948), p. 23.

Rákosi's policy of attrition—his famous "salami" tactics—proved irresistible. Although the Smallholder prime minister, Ferenc Nagy, wrote retrospectively that he counted the days until the peace treaty would be ratified and the occupation presumably ended, the race was an uneven one.[22] By the end of 1946 several Smallholder deputies had been expelled and arrested on charges of "fascist" and "reactionary" activities. In February of the following year the secretary general of the party, Béla Kovács, was arrested for his alleged role in a conspiracy against the Hungarian Republic. The final blow came when Ferenc Nagy, while on holiday in Switzerland, was advised that a "confession" by Kovács had implicated him in the conspiracy; his letter of resignation was exchanged for his child at the Swiss border. With most of their anticommunist leaders either in exile or in prison, the Smallholders ceased to be an effective government.[23]

It is arguable that the Smallholder leadership contributed to its own extinction by deliberately concealing from the nation the Soviet and communist pressures that were being continually exerted on it. Its reasons rested partly in the fear that confrontation might bring definitive retaliation, and partly in the somewhat wishful expectation that the imminent peace treaty would allow its political consolidation. An inherent weakness of the party had been that it attracted a wide range of noncommunist support which led to a lack of homogeneity and common resolve; some of its members, like István Dobi and Gyula Ortutay, sympathized more-or-less covertly with the communists.

[22] F. Nagy, *Struggle Behind the Iron Curtain,* p. 387.
[23] See *Fehér Könyu: A magyar köztársaság ás demokrácia elleni összeesküvés* (Budapest, 1947).

Nagy's putative successor, Dezső Sulyok, was vetoed by Rákosi and proceeded to found his own Freedom Party, which, together with Zoltán Pfeiffer's Hungarian Independence Party, István Barankovics' Democratic People's Party, and other splinter groups, attempted to rally the anticommunist vote.[24] This fragmented opposition was weakened by a new electoral law which in effect disfranchised numerous anticommunist voters and favored the now communist-dominated coalition. All the machinations and electoral frauds that surrounded the general elections of August, 1947, failed, however, to bring about a landslide for the communists, whose support rose to only 22 per cent of the total vote; the entire coalition polled 61 per cent. The final distribution of parliamentary seats gave 271 to the coalition parties (100 for the communists, 68 for the Smallholders, 67 for the Social Democrats, 36 for the National Peasants) and 140 to the various opposition groups.

The outcome of the election was significant not only in that it confirmed communist supremacy within the coalition and therefore in government, but also in that it definitively ruled out any further semidemocratic experiments by Rákosi. It should be noted that in all these elections the platforms of the noncommunist parties differed on few essential points; some, like the Barankovics Party and the Christian Women's League, were explicitly Catholic, but all supported the liberal reforms outlined by the original provisional government and all derived their electoral support from their opposition to the communists.

The next eighteen months saw the eradication of any

[24] A good sketch of the postwar political climate can be found in Desiderius Sulyok, *Zwei Nächte ohne Tag* (Zurich, 1948).

vestige of organized resistance to communist rule. The opposition parties were eliminated, as were those members of the coalition parties whose loyalty was suspect. Purges left the Social Democratic Party in the hands of its procommunist leader, Árpád Szakasits, and in June, 1948, this rump merged with the newly named Hungarian Workers' Party. By now the communists were remarkably candid regarding the sources of their power—the police and the Soviet military presence—and the superfluity of further pretense at parliamentary government.[25] All parties and mass organizations having been amalgamated into a People's Front, elections on a single-list basis were held in May, 1949, and brought to the Front fully 96.5 per cent of the votes cast. The newly elected National Assembly then proceeded to proclaim Hungary a People's Republic and to adopt a constitution modeled on that of the Soviet Union.[26]

The political system that prevailed in Hungary from 1949 onward was, like those in the other East European states, a dictatorship of the proletariat articulated by a single party, and consequently our analysis must begin with that nucleus.[27] The ideology of the Communist

[25] See, for instance, József Révai's essay "On the Character of Our People's Democracy," *Foreign Affairs,* 28 (1949) : 143-52.

[26] A republic had originally been proclaimed on February 1, 1946. The new constitution, promulgated on August 20, 1949 (intentionally on St. Stephen's Day), embodied lavish praise for the Red Army's role in the liberation of Hungary. It established a presidential council in lieu of a head of state, a council of ministers as the chief executive organ, and a unicameral national assembly; Article 56 in effect codified the dominant position of the Hungarian Workers' Party. The full text can be found in Jan F. Triska, *Constitutions of the Communist Party-States* (Stanford, Calif., 1968), pp. 182-94. Cf. Mátyás Rákosi, *A dolgozó nép alkotmánya* (Budapest, 1949), and Skilling, *Governments of Communist East Europe,* pp. 48ff.

[27] See Robert Gábor, *Organization and Strategy of the Hungarian Workers' Party,* 2d ed. rev. (New York, 1952).

Party, while ostensibly founded on Marxism-Le.
in this period amounted to a slavish imitation of t.
Stalinist prototype in the Soviet Union as expressed by
Rákosi and his closest advisers. Rákosi had been
Stalin's confidant in his Muscovite days and he subsequently never deviated from his mentor's precepts.
The hierarchical organization of the party followed the
Soviet pattern, with the pyramid rising from the local
councils through regional committees to the Central
Committee and the Politburo. The realities of power
were also similar. First Secretary Rákosi was the unquestioned leader, his unlimited prerogative being
shared to some extent by Gerő, Révai, and Farkas, who
were respectively in charge of the economy, culture
and agitprop, and defense. A triennial national party
congress had the function of ratifying decisions of the
Central Committee and of preparing long-term policy.
The first few years following the war had seen a determined drive to gain adherents, and, with the creation
of the Hungarian Workers' Party, membership hit an
estimated peak of 1,500,000.[28] By that time, however,
the new specter of Titoism had appeared, and the
members of the Cominform were warned that the
satellite parties must eliminate all factions and unreliable elements and become a truly monolithic vanguard.

Within the Hungarian Communist Party the first
major purge hit the leading non-Muscovite member of
the Politburo, onetime Minister of the Interior László
Rajk. Together with a number of other apparatchiks,
he confessed to a wide range of conspiratorial activities,
including Titoist deviationism, and was executed in
September, 1949.[29] The accusations leveled at Rajk

[28] Helmreich, *Hungary,* p. 126.
[29] Various hypotheses regarding the motivation behind Rajk's
purge are discussed in Paul Kecskeméti, *The Unexpected Revolution* (Stanford, Calif., 1961), pp. 18–31; an inside account is

69

were admitted to be pure fabrication at the time of his rehabilitation in 1956, but in 1949 his purge served as a slap in the face to Tito and as dissuasion to any proponents of national communism. In the ensuing purification campaign tens of thousands of party members and others were imprisoned, including leading Social Democrat collaborators György Marosán and Szakasits. In 1951 it was the turn of indigenous communists like Kádár, Gyula Kállai, Géza Losonczy, and Ferenc Donáth to be arrested; one estimate puts the total number of purge victims at two hundred thousand.[30] These purges, together with a moratorium on new admissions, pared party membership down to 862,114 in early 1951, although by the end of the following year a new recruitment policy brought it up again to a million. The end result was to leave a core of activists, loyal to Rákosi, surrounded by a relatively small opportunistic periphery.

Since, as we noted earlier, the internal integrative value of communist ideology in Hungary was negligible, the essential tasks of the new political system became the eradication of dissent and the mobilization of mass support. To promote these goals it developed an exceedingly high regulative capability which rested in the first instance on the secret police. Under the direction of the notorious Gábor Péter (who was himself purged in March, 1954), the AVH (State Security Authority) acquired a reputation for a ubiquitous

given by Vincent Savarius (pseudonym for Béla Szász), *Without Compulsion* (Brussels, 1963), while the official indictment can be found in *László Rajk and His Accomplices Before the People's Court* (Budapest, 1949).

[30] Zbigniew K. Brzezinski, "The Pattern of Political Purges," *The Annals of the American Academy of Political Science,* 317 (1958) : 84.

network of informers, detailed dossiers on virtually every citizen, and refined techniques of interrogation, all of which gave rise to an atmosphere of acute insecurity.[31] Assorted paramilitary organizations, workers' and young people's militia, and the people's army also contributed to the regulative capacity of the system, although they failed the loyalty test of the 1956 revolution.

The goal of political mobilization was less successfully fulfilled by the system, for at least in theory it requires a modicum of responsiveness which the regime lacked in the period under consideration. The absence of popular ideological motivation or sense of participation meant that, despite a high flow of symbolic outputs in the form of parades, mass rallies, and exhortative propaganda, the overwhelming majority of the population remained alienated and unconvinced of the regime's legitimacy. Nevertheless, the Communist Party fostered the growth of numerous mass organizations under the all-inclusive umbrella of the Patriotic People's Front. Acting on the assumption that young people were most susceptible to socialization into new behavior patterns, the regime launched in 1950 the DISZ (Federation of Working Youth) and a Pioneer movement aimed at younger children. DISZ membership hovered around 600,000, or approximately 35 per cent of the relevant age groups, while the Pioneers enrolled some 75 per cent of primary-school students.[32] Although both organizations were charged with indoctrination and were intended to prepare eventual recruits for the élite, subsequent events revealed that

[31] For details of the security apparatus, see Helmreich, *Hungary,* pp. 132–43.
[32] See *ibid.,* pp. 128–30.

71

the perceptible shift of the mass political culture to the left did not involve acceptance of the system's totalitarian features.

Centralized control extended not only to mass organizations; education and the entire communications structure also lost any autonomy that they had possessed and were put to the task of political indoctrination and cultural Russification. As we have seen, the churches' long-standing role in education was virtually eliminated along with all patriotic and Western-classical aspects of the curriculum. Instead, the period was characterized by the application of Stalin's version of Marxism-Leninism in every field of learning and by a strong bias in favor of specialized technical education at the secondary level which reflected the regime's economic priorities.[33] At the same time, the road to higher education was barred to all "class enemies," regardless of ability. Communications media were similarly placed under state direction and given a propagandistic function. Although these regulative and socializing measures allowed the system to maintain itself in the short run, the complete lack of channels for the articulation of popular demands created vast pools of resentment that ultimately found expression only in extreme anomic behavior.

In considering the allocative and extractive capabilities of the new political system, we must analyze postwar economic policies and in particular the applica-

[33] See Zbigniew K. Brzezinski, *The Soviet Bloc* (New York, 1961), p. 114. The distribution of university students by faculty indicated a stress on technological modernization. The most striking change occurred in law and engineering, which in 1938/39 accounted for 37.5 and 9.6 per cent of the total enrollment, whereas by 1949/50 the proportions were 9.1 and 28.9 per cent; see Helmreich, *Hungary*, p. 204.

tion and suitability of the Soviet development model. The first economic reform, the 1945 redistribution of farmland covering one-third of the area of Hungary, was obviously unrelated to that model; it was paradoxical that a communist minister of agriculture, Imre Nagy, should supervise a reform that by and large eliminated peasant discontent and therewith his party's chances for gaining rural support. The following table shows the change in the distribution of landholdings:[34]

	1935		1946	
	Percentage of farms	Percentage of total farming area	Percentage of farms	Percentage of total farming area
Dwarf farms	72.5	10.1	68.1	17.9
Small farms	12.5	9.2	18.8	21.1
Medium farms	13.3	26.1	11.9	32.0
Large farms	1.7	54.6	1.2	29.0
Total	100.0	100.0	100.0	100.0

This redistribution, however, did not solve all of the problems of Hungarian agriculture; although almost half of the population was still in the agricultural sector, the prewar methods of extensive cultivation did not suit the new proliferation of small farms. Most experts saw the solution in a switch to labor-intensive crops, an appropriate model being Danish agricul-

[34] Adapted from Balassa, *The Hungarian Experience in Economic Planning*, p. 245; many of the dwarf farms belonged to part-time cultivators.

ture.[35] The ideological preconceptions of the communist elite, however, and its mania for following Soviet practice, regardless of environmental differences, made the eventual collectivization campaign inevitable.

Aware of the widespread unpopularity of this prospect, Rákosi launched the campaign in low key in 1948, and accordingly the system grew very slowly. New pressure tactics brought membership in the collectives to a peak in 1952, when it accounted for 19.1 per cent of all agricultural workers; by that time the socialist sector in agriculture, including both state farms and collectives, accounted for a little more than one-third of all arable land. In theory this creation of larger farming units might have brought about certain economies of scale, if only in the use of agricultural machinery. However, the conjuncture of coercive tactics, high delivery quotas, unstable income flows, incompetent management, and the persecution of the kulak class had a disincentive effect which resulted in the stagnation of agricultural production. Despite a fairly constant balance of labor and capital inputs, the value of agricultural production fell in 1952 (at the height of the collectivization campaign) to 70 per cent of the 1938 level, 83 per cent of the 1949 level.

In the reconstruction period the primary objectives had been to stabilize the currency, which suffered from runaway inflation, and to restore the country's prewar production capacity. The program proved successful and was accompanied by the nationalization of certain industries; by mid-1947, the coal mines, the iron and steel industry, the electricity-generating in-

[35] *Ibid.*, pp. 244ff.; cf. Imre Kovács, *Agrárpolitikai feladatok* (Budapest, 1946), and Leland Stowe, "Hungary's Agrarian Revolution," *Foreign Affairs,* 25 (1947) : 490–502.

dustry, and the major banks and their dependent enterprises had been nationalized, which, together with previously state-owned concerns, brought to 50 per cent the proportion of the industrial and transport working force employed by the state. The Three-Year Plan that covered the period 1947–49 aimed to increase investment and industrial production, but it consisted of general directives that stopped far short of the Soviet model.[36] Halfway through the life of the plan the Hungarian People's Republic came into being, and concurrently the socialization of the economy was accelerated. By the end of 1949 every enterprise with ten or more employees had been nationalized, bringing to 99 per cent the proportion of nonagricultural workers in the state sector. Official and independent estimates put the resulting increase in the national income over 1938 levels at anywhere from 16 per cent to 24 per cent; the plan promoted a remarkable recovery, considering the state of the economy in 1945, and the standard of living almost reached prewar levels.[37]

With the inception of the first Five-Year Plan in 1950, the Stalinist model found indiscriminate application both in the agricultural sector, where collectivization was launched, and in the industrial sector, which was singled out for intensive development.[38] Fully 86 per cent of investments in industry were earmarked for heavy industry in order to turn Hungary into a "country of iron and steel." Since Hungary must im-

[36] See George Kemény, *Economic Planning in Hungary, 1947–49* (London, 1952).

[37] Balassa, *The Hungarian Experience in Economic Planning*, pp. 30–31; cf. Zoltán Vas, "The Completion of the Three-Year Plan: A Victory for Our People," *Társadalmi Szemle*, 5, no. 3 (1950) : 131–51.

[38] *The Five Year Plan of the Hungarian People's Republic* (Budapest, 1950).

port 90 per cent of her coking coal and 80 per cent of her iron ore, the creation of a great iron and steel complex such as that at Sztalinváros can only be explained in terms of the regime's ideological-autarchic preconceptions. Positive aspects of the Five-Year Plan were a growth rate in the national income of 5.6 per cent between 1949 and 1955, as well as a state of full employment, but indigenous and foreign experts have since agreed that these were far outweighed by the negative consequences. The notable increase in the growth rate was achieved at the cost of a disproportionately high rate of investment, particularly in heavy industry, and the gross neglect of other (and potentially more productive) sectors of the economy; the high savings ratio resulted in an 18 per cent *drop* in the real incomes of workers and employees between 1949 and 1952.[39] In that same period the labor force in industry and mining and smelting increased by 370,000, the rapid transfer aggravating the already low productivity of the uncooperative peasantry.[40] The neglect of agriculture and of the light industries and handicraft trades had a negative effect both on consumer satisfaction and on Hungary's trading strength. In almost every respect, therefore, the massive industrialization program of the regime proved to be ill-conceived and retrogressive.

[39] Balassa, *The Hungarian Experience in Economic Planning,* pp. 31–35, 216ff.; cf. Ernő Gerő, *The Position of the Hungarian National Economy in 1952* (Budapest, 1952).

[40] Helmreich, *Hungary,* p. 71. The influx of industrial workers to the capital aggravated the already chronic housing shortage, although the problem was partially resolved by deporting expendable "class enemies" to remote villages. It must also be noted that employment was not always voluntary; see Richard K. Carlton *et al., Forced Labor in the "People's Democracies"* (New York, 1955).

Integration—From the Axis to the Cominform

While Hungary achieved a degree of independent control over internal matters in the pluralistic inter-regnum after 1945, she never recovered her freedom of action in foreign relations, which remained narrowly circumscribed by the emerging East-West cleavage and by the Soviet Union's ideological and strategic orientations. When on December 30, 1944, a second Hungarian armistice delegation representing the De-brecen government assembled in Moscow, it was quickly made to understand that its role was merely to accept a Russian *Diktat*. As early as March, 1943, Anthony Eden had observed that Stalin's dislike for Hungarians would produce harsh peace terms, and the armistice agreement that was signed on January 20, 1945, proved him right.[41] It nullified the Vienna Awards, committed Hungary to a declaration of war on Germany, and stipulated reparations of $200,000,000 for the Soviet Union and $100,000,000 for Czechoslovakia and Yugoslavia to be paid in commodities over a period of six years; the Allied Control Commission, charged with the task of supervising the execution of the armistice terms, was participated in nominally by Britain and the United States but was placed under the "general direction" of the Soviet High Command.

The Americans had expressed reservations regarding these terms; on the territorial question, for instance, their preference was for a more equitable ethnic settlement, particularly in Transylvania. A compromise of sorts was reached in the Rumanian armistice agree-

[41] Robert E. Sherwood, *Roosevelt and Hopkins* (New York, 1948), p. 711. For the text of the armistice agreement, see World Peace Foundation, *Documents on American Foreign Relations, 1944–1945,* pp. 244–50.

ment, which specified that Transylvania "or the great part thereof" should be annexed to Rumania, subject to confirmation at the final peace settlement.[42] In the course of the Allied discussions Molotov reminded his interlocutors that the presence of the Red Army in these areas was sufficient warrant for any Soviet action.[43] The U.S. State Department's assessment prior to Yalta of the "Principal Hungarian Problems" was prophetic: "It is possible that Soviet and American policy may not be in harmony if the Soviet Union uses its position as the power in actual control of the execution of the armistice to intervene in Hungarian domestic affairs, to dominate Hungary, or to pursue a severe policy on the reparation question which would cripple Hungarian economy. . . ."[44] It listed as desirable principles maximum Western participation in the Allied Control Commission, a reparation policy consistent with economic recovery, and territorial settlements that would "rectify the frontier with Rumania in favor of Hungary on ethnic grounds" and "transfer to Hungary some of the predominantly Hungarian-populated districts of southern Slovakia." However, the paper made equally clear that these principles would not lead the United States to take the position of supporting Hungary against the Soviet Union, and, in the event, the Declaration on Liberated Europe turned out to have a purely hortatory function.[45]

The postwar status of Hungary was only a by-prod-

[42] World Peace Foundation, *Documents on American Foreign Relations, 1944–1945,* p. 235.

[43] Herbert Feis, *Churchill, Roosevelt, Stalin* (Princeton, 1957) , p. 548.

[44] U.S., Department of State, *The Conferences at Malta and Yalta,* pp. 242–45.

[45] Originally, the plans had included an emergency high commission for liberated Europe which would supervise the appli-

uce of the long series of Allied negotiations stretching from Potsdam through the Council of Foreign Ministers' meetings to the Paris Peace Conference, which, in the main, lie outside the scope of this study. The Western position regarding implementation of the wartime undertakings concerning Eastern Europe hardened as the months went by but failed to inhibit Soviet activities in Hungary, and the Allied Control Commission, despite repeated American protests, functioned as an unfettered extension of the Soviet High Command.[46] As a result, Soviet policies regarding internal politics, the modalities of reparations, and territorial questions prevailed without effective Western interference. Shortly before the 1945 general elections, both the United States and the Soviet Union re-established formal diplomatic relations with Hungary in an attempt to bolster the popularity of the respectively pro-Western and procommunist members of the coalition.[47] Although it is unlikely that these ploys affected the outcome of the election, it is fair to say that the initial foreign orientation of the new Hungarian government was one of accommodation toward both the Soviet Union and the Western Powers, with

---

cation of the declaration's principles, but Roosevelt dismissed the idea on the grounds that a new world organization and regular meetings of foreign ministers could better deal with the issue. U.S., Department of State, *Postwar Foreign Policy Preparation, 1939–1945* (Washington, D.C., 1949), pp. 372–73, 394, and 655–57; cf. Edward R. Stettinius, *Roosevelt and the Russians: The Yalta Conference* (New York, 1950), pp. 68, 87.

[46] See Stephen D. Kertész, *Diplomacy in a Whirlpool* (Notre Dame, Ind., 1953), pp. 110 and *passim,* and H. F. A. Schoenfeld, "Soviet Imperialism in Hungary," *Foreign Affairs,* 26, no. 2 (1948) : 554–66. At the time, Kertész was a senior Hungarian diplomat; Schoenfeld, the American minister to Hungary.

[47] U.S., Department of State, *A Decade of American Foreign Policy: Basic Documents, 1941–49* (Washington, D.C., 1950), p. 501; cf. Kertész, *Diplomacy in a Whirlpool,* p. 113.

a view to the re-establishment at the eventual peace conference of a sovereignty unqualified by military occupation.

Increasing Soviet pressures, either direct or by the intermediation of the Communist Party, placed severe restraints on the freedom of the post-1945 government to pursue Hungarian interests on the international level; and since its perception of Hungary's interests largely coincided with the popular consensus, its failures had the further effect of eroding electoral support. In the economic sphere the government found itself unable to prevent the extension of Soviet control. Apart from the reparation payments, which in 1947 accounted for 26.4 per cent of the budget, the Potsdam Agreement transferring German assets to the Soviet Union was interpreted by the latter to include property seized by the Germans during the war as well as Hungarian debts to Germany. This led in part to the establishment of six Soviet-Hungarian companies (notably in the fields of transportation and bauxite extraction), thus creating an economic link that invariably worked to the advantage of the dominant partner.[48] It has been estimated that in the period from 1945 to 1956 the net profit derived by the Soviet Union from these various operations in Hungary amounted to one billion dollars.[49]

In the matter of territorial settlements, the government labored under the double handicap of Hungary's ex-enemy status and a Soviet policy which favored the successor states. An *ad hoc* government, predominantly

[48] Nicholas Spulber, *The Economics of Communist Eastern Europe* (Cambridge, Mass., 1957), p. 188.

[49] J. Wszelaki, *Communist Economic Strategy: The Role of East Central Europe* (Washington, D.C., 1959), pp. 68ff.; cf. Howard J. Hilton, Jr., "Hungary: A Case History of Soviet Economic Imperialism," *Department of State Bulletin*, August 25, 1951, pp. 323-27.

Magyar and procommunist, materialized in Kolozsvár
(Cluj) in late 1943, and apparently for a while the
Soviet Union contemplated establishing an independent Transylvania, but this turned out to be a
divide et impera tactic which evaporated when Petru
Groza succeeded in implanting a communist regime
in Bucharest.[50] The Soviet Union was determined to
keep Bessarabia, which it had annexed in 1940, but
saw no advantage in defending Hungarian claims to
Transylvania. Another bone of contention was the
Hungarian minority in Slovakia. One of the wartime
understandings between Beneš and Stalin had been
the expulsion of this minority, which Beneš considered
to be unreliable and a threat to the Czechoslovakian
national state. As a first step, in 1945 the Czechoslovak
government confiscated all land owned by Hungarians
(and Germans) and issued a number of other discriminatory decrees.[51] The Budapest regime sent to the
Allied Control Commission a flurry of notes protesting
this persecution but failed to elicit more than an American condemnation of the collective punishment of
ethnic minority groups.[52] The Czechs then came forward with a proposal for a population exchange which

[50] See Burks, *Dynamics of Communism in Eastern Europe,*
pp. 56–57, and Ferenc A. Váli, "Transylvania and the Hungarian Minority," *Journal of International Affairs,* 20, no. 1
(1966) : 32–44.

[51] Josef Korbel, *The Communist Subversion of Czechoslo-
vakia, 1938–1948* (Princeton, 1959) , p. 161; cf. Eduard Taborsky,
"Beneš and Stalin—Moscow, 1943 and 1945," *Journal of Central
European Affairs,* 13 (1953) : 168, and Hungary, Külügyminisz-
térium, *Hungary and the Conference of Paris,* vols. 2 and 4
(Budapest, 1947) , 4:176–86.

[52] Britain and the United States rejected Hungarian requests
that an international commission be set up to investigate the
plight of Magyar minorities. See Kertész, *Diplomacy in a Whirlpool,* p. 122 and app., doc. 12, 13, 14; see also *Hungary and the
Conference of Paris,* 2:155-63.

had the enthusiastic support of Stalin (although concurrently the Russians were assuring Rákosi of the contrary),[53] and an agreement was signed in February, 1946; neither the exchange, nor the deportation of many Hungarians to the Sudetenland, nor the continuing discrimination against the remaining minority, nor the unexceptionable Czech view that Hungary had taken advantage of the Munich settlement, contributed to amicable relations between the two countries.

As the date of the peace conference approached, the Hungarian government intensified its efforts to reach an acceptable compromise on the territorial issues.[54] Stalin, meeting a delegation headed by Prime Minister Ferenc Nagy, ostensibly agreed with their protests regarding the Slovakian Magyars; on the question of Transylvania, Molotov urged the Hungarians to negotiate directly with Groza. But it soon became apparent that neither of them had any intention of reconsidering the matter,[55] and at the meeting of the Council of Foreign Ministers in Paris in May, 1945, the award of all Transylvania to Rumania was made explicit.

Hungary's peace aims were first presented to the Allies in a note dated August 14, 1945, which proposed, *inter alia,* institutions to implement Danubian economic cooperation and a solution to the territorial problem based on ethnic self-determination.[56] The only significant reaction was the strongly critical one of the Soviet Union, which hinted that the Eastern Europeans

[53] See Korbel, *Communist Subversion of Czechoslovakia,* pp. 179–80.

[54] See Hungary, Külügyminisztérium, *Le problème hongrois par rapport à la Roumanie, Le problème hongrois par rapport à la Tchécoslovaquie,* and *Le problème de la minorité hongroise de Slovaquie* (Budapest, 1946).

[55] F. Nagy, *Struggle Behind the Iron Curtain,* pp. 209–10, 219, 227.

[56] See Kertész, *Diplomacy in a Whirlpool,* pp. 163–87.

were ideologically not ready for this type of community-building. Following a visit to Hungary early in 1946, a British parliamentary delegation reported that "a dictate like the Treaty of Trianon should be avoided, and a full opportunity for consultation should be afforded to Hungary and her neighbours if a just and lasting peace is to be established"; concurrently, Secretary of State Byrnes recorded that a number of American proposals were being made to reduce reparations and to ensure freedom of navigation on the Danube.[57] Despite this sympathy, Soviet opposition to Hungary's stated interests ensured that no meaningful negotiations would take place. What one American observer referred to as the Soviet-led "Slav bloc" prevailed over Western and Hungarian objections,[58] and the only new product of the conference was the transfer of the Magyar-populated "Bratislava bridgehead" to Czechoslovakia; a somewhat paradoxical proposal from Prague to expel 200,000 Hungarians was defeated. The peace treaty embodied a number of clauses recommending respect for human rights and political self-determination, but the lack of effective supervision made these of nominal value, while the clause allowing occupation troops to remain to guard communication lines, pending an Austrian settlement, ensured that Hungary would remain within the Soviet sphere of influence.[59]

[57] Great Britain, Parliament, All-Party Delegation to Hungary, *Unanimous Report on Hungary* (London, 1946); James F. Byrnes, *Speaking Frankly* (New York, 1947), pp. 130, 148–49.

[58] Philip E. Mosely, "Peace-Making, 1946," *International Organization,* 1, no. 1 (1946): 22–32; cf. Stephen D. Kertész, "Reflections on Soviet and American Negotiating Behavior," *Review of Politics,* 19, no. 1 (1957): 20–23.

[59] It later transpired that the Czech plan to expel the Hungarians was related to the expected transfer of Germans from Hungary; see Michael Hogye, *The Paris Peace Conference of 1946: Role of the Hungarian Communists and of the Soviet*

The internal consequences of the government's failure to achieve even the minimum of Hungary's goals are difficult to estimate; the Smallholder Party undoubtedly suffered a loss in prestige, but the role of the Communist Party as an advocate of Soviet policies and its inability or unwillingness to bring those policies into closer conformity with Hungarian interests did not add to its popularity. In any event, Hungarian initiatives in external affairs were becoming more and more circumscribed both by internal political developments and by the Soviet Union's resolve to consolidate her wartime gains into an impregnable buffer zone. When Hungary was invited to send a delegate to Paris in June, 1947, to discuss Secretary of State Marshall's proposed aid program, Prime Minister Dinnyés' initial reaction was favorable and he consulted the Allied Control Commission, but, as in the case of the other East European countries, the Soviet Union vetoed Hungarian participation.[60] By the following summer Budapest's subservience to Moscow could no longer be doubted. Although Hungary had consistently endorsed the principle of freedom of navigation on the Danube (first codified in 1856) and had been recommending international control over the waterway, she joined the Soviet Union at the Belgrade Conference of 1948 in support of a convention that restricted membership on the governing commission to riparian states, thus in effect ensuring Soviet domination of the Danubian

Union (New York, 1954), p. 2. Cf. U.S., Department of State, _Paris Peace Conference, 1946: Selected Documents_ (Washington, D.C., 1947), pp. 1016–42, 1063–64, 1104–5, 1123, 1194–95; John C. Campbell, "The European Territorial Settlement," _Foreign Affairs,_ 26, no. 1 (1948): 214, 218; and Harold Nicolson, "Peacemaking in Paris: Success, Failure or Farce?" _Foreign Affairs,_ 25, no. 2 (1947): 198.

[60] Stephen D. Kertész, ed., _The Fate of East-Central Europe_ (Notre Dame, Ind., 1956), p. 239.

system; the convention, signed on August 18, was not recognized by the Western participants.[61] Andrei Zhdanov's separation of the world into "two camps," enunciated at the Cominform's founding convention in September, 1947, had ruled out the middle course upon which most realistic Hungarians had based their hopes.

The period of intensive socialization saw the rapid integration of Hungary into the Stalinist system.[62] Once the Communist Party and the state had merged into a single nucleus of political power, no further obstacles were encountered by policy directives from the Kremlin. The process of integration was characterized less by treaties and formalized diplomatic links than by personal and semiofficial forms of communication and control. The most important of these proved to be the relationship between Rákosi and Stalin, for the former adulated the latter, sinned only in the excess of his efforts to comply with Stalin's wishes, and transposed to Hungary the same "cult of personality" that prevailed in the Soviet Union; in addition, occasional consultations on the party-delegation level served to strengthen these cooperative links. The Soviet presence in Budapest, of equal importance in coordinating Hungarian politics, ranged from the ambassador and his staff through the High Command of the occupation forces to the Soviet agents who operated parallel to Hungarian functionaries in the secret police and in the more sensitive ministries, such as defense. The full extent of this Soviet tutelage was to become evident at the time of the New Course, when even Rákosi would be ignominiously demoted on Moscow's initiative.

Integration in the Stalinist period was also distin-

[61] John C. Campbell, "Diplomacy on the Danube," *Foreign Affairs,* 27, no. 1 (1949) : 315–37.

[62] For a general discussion of this system and its evolution, see Brzezinski, *The Soviet Bloc,* chap. 6.

guished by the prevalence of bilateral over multilateral links, an outcome of the same Soviet determination to destroy regional bonds which earlier had led to the rejection of Hungarian proposals for Danubian cooperation. Imre Nagy later referred to the isolation of the East European fragments, not only from the West, but also from each other, by "a veritable Chinese Wall."[63] Consultations were carried on between Moscow and the individual people's democracies and only seldom among the latter. Although the Cominform started out as the central agency for multilateral political coordination (ostensibly as a riposte to the Marshall Plan and other Western efforts at cooperation), it never really became a forum for consultation but rather evolved into a less and less active channel for the dissemination of anti-Tito propaganda. Of similarly symbolic value were the various treaties of friendship and mutual aid concluded between Hungary and the Soviet Union, Poland, Czechoslovakia, Bulgaria, Rumania, and East Germany from 1948 to 1950.[64] In the case of Czechoslovakia and Rumania the treaties did nothing to resolve the old contentious issues, but the Soviet policy of playing down historical rivalries

[63] Imre Nagy, *On Communism: In Defense of the New Course* (New York, 1957), p. 240.

[64] The treaties were bilateral precursors of the Warsaw Pact in that they all stressed common defense against Germany and the West; other clauses enjoined respect for each other's sovereignty and recommended economic and cultural cooperation. Hungary signed the treaty with the Soviet Union on February 18, 1948; that with Rumania on January 24, 1948; with Poland on June 18, 1948; with Bulgaria on July 16, 1948; with Czechoslovakia on April 16, 1949; and with East Germany on June 26, 1950. For the resolution setting out the aims of the Cominform, see Robert H. McNeal, ed., *International Relations Among Communists* (Englewood Cliffs, N.J., 1967), pp. 54–56; cf. Adam B. Ulam, "The Cominform and the People's Democracies," *World Politics,* 3, no. 1 (1951) : 200–217.

and ethnic friction indirectly improved the lot of the Transylvanian Hungarians, who by the Rumanian Constitution of 1952 were granted an autonomous province and certain cultural rights.[65] (Yugoslavia also concluded a bilateral treaty with Hungary in 1947, but the Stalin-Tito schism soon made it meaningless and Rákosi became Tito's most vociferous enemy.) All these formal links were the symbols rather than the instruments of Hungary's political absorption into the Soviet system.

The Stalinist patterns of integration were reflected as well in the postwar evolution of Hungary's economic links. We have already touched on the extension of Soviet control over parts of the economy by means of joint companies formed after the 1945 treaty of economic cooperation. Through its claim to German assets, the Soviet Union also gained control of the Hungarian Credit Bank, and when the banking system was subsequently overhauled, this institution became the only source of industrial credit. It was presumably confidence in the stability of the system that led the Kremlin to transfer sixty-nine Soviet enterprises to the Hungarian government in 1952; a further agreement two years later covered the Soviet shares in the joint-stock companies, but the uranium mines remained under direct Soviet management.[66]

[65] Váli, "Transylvania and the Hungarian Minority." The Rumanian regime claimed that "only the victory of the People's Democracy brought a solution of the national question and the establishment of national peace in Transylvania" (*Scinteia,* January 22, 1948, quoted in Kazimierz Grzybowski, *The Socialist Commonwealth of Nations* [New Haven, Conn., 1964], p. 215).

[66] See Grzybowski, *Socialist Commonwealth of Nations,* pp. 42–48. In 1948, in order to strengthen the Rákosi regime, the Soviet Union reduced the outstanding balance of the reparations and extended the repayment time to eight years.

Apart from these largely exploitative arrangements, the beginnings of economic integration could be found in a few bilateral agreements and in the creation in January, 1949, of the Council for Mutual Economic Assistance (CEMA), of which Hungary was a founding member. In 1947 Hungary and Yugoslavia signed two agreements, one for economic cooperation, the other for a joint stock corporation to develop a bauxite-aluminum industry in Yugoslavia, but for obvious reasons neither agreement bore fruit. Hungary and Rumania agreed in 1952 to coordinate the development of their chemical industries, while in 1954 the same two countries plus Bulgaria decided to cooperate in the light industrial sector.[67]

Neither these agreements nor the establishment of the CEMA, however, led to extensive economic cooperation and coordinated specialization. An attempt was made to rationalize trade relations in 1951 when the CEMA Secretariat issued a set of general rules and regulations, but this had little effect on the patterns of economic development in Eastern Europe. In practice the Soviet Union controlled the terms of trade, and only infrequently was development in the individual countries determined by any local advantages in the factors of production, such as when the Korean war occasioned a certain degree of coordination in the production of military supplies leading to the Hungarian specialization in communications equipment.[68]

As we saw earlier, the period of intensive socialization was notable for its indiscriminate application of the Soviet model in the East European countries, where autarchic theories became the current orthodoxy. Hungary, being poorly endowed in most raw materials,

[67] *Ibid.*, pp. 53, 56–57.
[68] See *ibid.*, pp. 57–70.

proved a particularly unsuitable subject for this type of development. An economist who witnessed this phase later observed that the progressive deterioration of Hungary's trading position was brought about by a conjunction of "unsatisfactory production results in agriculture, forced development of import-intensive heavy industry, and insufficiency of investments and technological change in labor-intensive industries."[69] Clearly, only a high degree of specialization and productivity could make Hungary's nonagricultural exports economical and competitive; but concentration on heavy industry in the Rákosi period was marked by managerial and production inefficiencies that also afflicted the state trading agencies. The resultant trading weakness was balanced by drastic reduction in nonessential imports, mainly consumer goods, and these measures led to a favorable balance of trade in the period in question (except for 1949 and 1952); the balance of trade with the Soviet bloc as a whole was invariably favorable, while the opposite applied with respect to Hungary's trade with all other countries. This positive but limited achievement was further qualified by the fact that in the same period the balance-of-payments deficit mounted steadily as a result of various debts and obligations, many of them incurred vis à vis the Soviet Union under conditions of doubtful legitimacy.[70]

The degree of Hungary's integration into the Soviet system is made clear by the reorientation of her trade toward the bloc. In contrast to the prewar pattern noted in the preceding chapter, by 1950 the Soviet bloc accounted for 56.3 per cent of her imports and 64.7 per

[69] Balassa, *The Hungarian Experience in Economic Planning*, p. 270 and app. C., *passim*.
[70] *Ibid.*, pp. 275–76.

cent of her exports, the figures for the Soviet Union alone being 24.5 and 28.9 per cent.[71] (In that same year trade with Yugoslavia was nonexistent due to the economic boycott.) As will be seen, this pattern has prevailed, with relatively minor fluctuations, up to the present day. The Soviet Union replaced Germany as Hungary's dominant trading partner, while in 1950 Austria became her largest single noncommunist partner, controlling only 5.4 per cent of her trade.

The industrialization program was reflected also in the changing composition of Hungarian trade.[72] Imports of fuels and raw materials rose substantially to fulfill the needs of the new heavy industries, and there occurred a concurrent but slight increase in the export of machinery and precision products. The Soviet bloc provided all of the coking coal and the Soviet Union supplied 85 per cent of the iron ore that Hungary imported in 1950; on the export side, the Soviet Union accounted for more than 90 per cent of the outflow of bauxite.[73] Food exports, on the other hand, fell below 1938 levels and imports of noncomestible consumer goods suffered a spectacular drop from 32.3 per cent in 1938 to 2.7 per cent in 1949, a change that was not compensated for by any increase in domestic production.[74]

In sum, a major economic reorientation had taken place which imposed the Soviet development model and a new set of trading relationships on Hungary; however, this period of intensive socialization saw

[71] *MSZ, 1968,* pp. 96–97.
[72] See Balassa, *The Hungarian Experience in Economic Planning,* p. 267.
[73] *MSZ, 1968,* pp. 100–108.
[74] Balassa, *The Hungarian Experience in Economic Planning,* p. 267.

little tangible progress toward economic cooperation and the coordination of national plans among the East European states.

It should be clear from the foregoing analysis that the process of integration into the Stalinist system did not have the consensual support of Hungarian society and did not bring material benefits commensurate with the sacrifices that the economic planners had demanded. The political aspects of integration similarly lacked an indigenous base, for most Hungarians felt that their leaders were utterly subservient to Moscow and neglectful of such national goals as the settlement of territorial and ethnic claims. The perpetuation of the latter problem preserved an element of incompatibility which the élite could momentarily ignore but which was a potential obstacle to further regional integration. This total lack of benefits made any popular identification with the Soviet system unlikely, although the regulative capability of the regime and the retrenchment of the West into a posture of containment ruled out any internal movement toward radical changes in the status quo. It is difficult to estimate to what extent the political élite was motivated by considerations of personal power and prestige and by the very bourgeois perquisites of office, and to what extent it was possessed of ideological convictions that could ignore or rationalize the immediate costs of achieving communism. The personality of Stalin was more immediately relevant than any such speculation, and his passing from the scene occasioned a momentary turmoil that did not fail to reach deep into the Hungarian system.

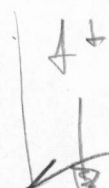

4: THAW AND REVOLUTION, 1953–57

Although the period of intensive socialization had been marked by different methods and rates of progress in accordance with local parameters and idiosyncratic leadership, by the end of 1952 the East European system had, with the notable exception of Yugoslavia, reached a state of institutional and ideological homogeneity which proved unattainable in subsequent years. A degree of consensual integration existed at the élite level, but, as we noted in the last chapter, this was manifested more in common subservience to Moscow than in genuinely multilateral forms of coordination and cooperation. The system now became subjected to new pressures, internal as well as external, which in the long run exerted a diversifying and disintegrative influence. From the United States came rumblings of discontent with the policy of containment and the implicit recognition of the Soviet sphere of influence, a discontent that acquired its most tangible form in the "liberation" platform of the Republican Party in the 1952 elections. Eisenhower's victory and the rather ambiguous pronouncements of his secretary of state, John Foster Dulles, contributed to the illusion of an American commitment to extricate the satellites from the Kremlin's grasp and encouraged U.S. propaganda organs to capitalize on the already endemic popular discontent in Eastern Europe. Of more immediate consequence was the hiatus in Soviet leadership which followed Stalin's death in March, 1953. His intensely personal political style and the personal loyalty he drew, most strikingly from Rákosi, were bound to create problems of readjustment in the period of transition.

Internal Factors in the Thaw

We have already noted some of the social and economic consequences of the application of the Stalinist model in Hungary. Imre Nagy, the man who became identified with the New Course, wrote in his *post facto* "dissertation":

> The "left-wing" deviationists, primarily Rákosi and Gerő, in the years 1949 to 1953 brought the socialist reorganization of agriculture to a dead end, bankrupted agricultural production, destroyed the worker-peasant alliance, undermined the power of the People's Democracy, trampled upon the rule of law, debased the people's living standards, established a rift between the masses and the Party and government—in other words swept the country towards catastrophe.[1]

That Nagy, a veteran communist and Muscovite, could view his party's performance in this light gives an inkling of the feelings of that vast majority of Hungarians who did not even have the comfort of ideological conviction. As early as 1948, Nagy had manifested a "right oppositionist" bias in claiming that Lenin's NEP policy was more suitable to the transitional stage

[1] I. Nagy, *On Communism*, p. 194.

94

of Hungary's evolution toward communism than the orthodox Stalinist model. His reward was expulsion from the Politburo and relegation to a teaching position at a provincial agricultural college. By the end of 1952 the concurrent party purges conducted by Rákosi had rid the political élite of ideological cleavages.

This homogenization of the élite's belief system found no parallel in the mass political culture. Historically, Hungarians had been singularly unreceptive to ideologies lacking a national foundation, and the imposition of an atheistic and alien dogma by the Russians and by a predominantly Jewish élite inevitably met with popular resistance. In spite of this negative predisposition, a reform program aimed at improving the peasants' and industrial workers' living standards might well have brought about a modicum of support for the political system; instead, the oppressive costs of socialization in terms of individual liberty and material well-being resulted in the alienation of the masses.

Research into the pattern of atomization of Hungarian society in this period has shown that white-collar and industrial workers were most affected; they were generally unaware of, and unresponsive to, the purely political aspects of the system, and their attitude could best be described as one of apathy.[2] Modifications in the organization of the agricultural sector resulted in widespread opposition among the peasantry, and this was materially reflected in the decline of agricultural productivity.[3] The amorphous group that constituted the intelligentsia was less atomized and more given to

[2] Kecskeméti, *The Unexpected Revolution*, pp. 84–91.
[3] See Harris L. Coulter, "The Hungarian Peasantry: 1948–1956," *The American Slavic and East European Review*, 18, no. 4 (1959) : 539–54.

95

political discussions on the individual level, and even among children there was a detectable pattern of un-receptiveness to political indoctrination. Thus, despite the regime's efforts at political socialization, the imposition of a dogmatic belief system met with little success and with a great deal of resistance that was passive and fragmented for want of institutionalized channels of articulation.

The potential explosiveness of this state of anomie was also brought out by a contemporary study of public opinion in Eastern Europe based on information provided by escapees in the years 1951 and 1952.[4] Although political *émigrés* are seldom entirely representative and are given to hyperbolic judgments, in this case subsequent events provided ample verification of their views. One significant finding, therefore, was that there existed in Hungary a very real hope for a war of liberation. As one young refugee observed, "Everyone wants war. . . . It doesn't pay to live like this anyway, being afraid all the time of what would happen the next night."[5] The popular consensus seemed to be that by virtue of the irreconcilability of the two camps —and Leninist dogma was invoked as proof—war was inevitable, and on this premise listeners tended to give Western broadcasts their selective attention in order to have their hopes for liberation reinforced. When the New Course was under way in 1954, for instance, Radio Free Europe launched Operation FOCUS, a massive radio and balloon-leaflet campaign which aimed to demoralize party functionaries by publicizing their misdeeds and which tried to spread the idea of a "National Opposition Movement" and its twelve demands

4 S. Kracauer and P. L. Berkman, *Satellite Mentality* (New York, 1956).

5 *Ibid.,* p. 155.

for economic and political reform.[6] The conjunc
of this propaganda campaign and an already alienated
and selective audience crystallized a shared, if unartic-
ulated, belief system that stood in contradistinction
to the values of the political élite. Nevertheless, as long
as that élite remained cohesive, the regulative capability of the system was adequate to contain internal
disaffection.

The New Course—External Determinants and Internal Consequences

To the hard core of orthodox Stalinists around Rákosi it was a matter of indifference that the masses were
alienated and hostile, for in their view the transition to
socialism necessarily entailed such sacrifices. When the
personification of this dogmatic view passed away, however, the orthodoxy at once came under attack. In
Moscow a new era of collective leadership was ushered
in by Malenkov; socialist legality, a more balanced
pattern of economic development, and an easing of
world tensions became some of the slogans of Stalin's
successors. The decision to abandon economic Stalinism came none too soon, judging by the East German
uprising in June, 1953, and the earlier riots in
Pilsen.

In Hungary, where industrialization had been carried out more extensively and with greater brutality
than in any other East European country,[7] the begin-

---

[6] Robert T. Holt, *Radio Free Europe* (Minneapolis, 1958),
pp. 162ff. Balloons also carried "Liberty Bell" medals with the
inscription "Hungarians for Freedom—All the Free World for
the Hungarians."

[7] See I. Nagy, *On Communism,* p. 185.

ning of de-Stalinization set off a disintegrative process
that culminated in open revolt. At a critical meeting in
Moscow in June, 1953, Soviet leaders took turns berat-
ing Rákosi, most vehemently for his economic misman-
agement. Beria allegedly accused Rákosi of having
acted like a "Jewish king," while Khrushchev warned
him that in the absence of speedy reforms he would be
"booted out summarily" by the Hungarian people; he
was thereupon ordered to relinquish the premiership
to Imre Nagy.[8] The shift to collective leadership, with
Nagy as prime minister and Rákosi remaining as the
party boss, created an anomalous situation in which the
former's ideological revisionism, sanctioned by Moscow,
was countered at every turn by the dogmatism of the
latter, who retained the allegiance of most of the apparat. For the first time since 1948 the Hungarian
political system had two competing power centers.

In Budapest the Central Committee met and approved a number of Nagy's reforms, which came to be
known as the "June resolutions." Rákosi, however,
prevailed in preventing their publication, and Nagy
presented instead a somewhat watered-down New
Course program to the National Assembly on July 4.[9] Its
main points aimed to curb the excesses of the period of
intensive socialization. Nagy announced that the most
important task of his new economic policy was to be "a
substantial all-round reduction, in accordance with the
capacity of the country, of the pace of development of
the national economy and of the investments." Deploring past attempts at autarchy, he declared that priority
would shift from heavy industry to light industries and
the production of consumer goods, and he went on to

---

[8] *Ibid.*, p. 66, and Tibor Méray, *Thirteen Days that Shook the
Kremlin* (London, 1959), p. 7.

[9] Royal Institute of International Affairs, *Documents on International Affairs, 1953* (London, 1956), pp. 177–81.

promise that the government would "permit the winding up of cooperative farms, where the majority of the membership wishes it." In addition to these economic pronouncements, Nagy stated that, whereas in the past the authorities had "often disregarded the provisions of the Constitution which safeguard the rights, liberties and securities of the citizen," his administration would show greater religious tolerance, abolish the internment camps, declare an amnesty for minor offenses, and revise the sentences of persons "who had been wronged." The last, needless to say, did not include anticommunists.

The alternative presented by the New Course was a radical departure from the policies of Rákosi; in all likelihood the Russian leaders hoped to preserve political stability in Hungary by balancing Rákosi the sectarian Stalinist against the reform-minded but loyal Nagy. In the event, however, the dual leadership degenerated into a tug of war which could only be arbitrated by the Kremlin itself. Of the two protagonists, Nagy felt that he had received a mandate from the Soviet leaders to implement his reforms, while Rákosi perceived the fragility of the consensus around Malenkov and decided to temporize. Some of Rákosi's fears were justified, for hardly had the New Course been announced than peasants began to leave collective farms and to distribute land on their own initiative. On July 11, encouraged by the arrest of his chief critic, Beria, Rákosi made a speech full of veiled threats against those who would misinterpret the reforms; he attacked the kulaks (Nagy had decided to discontinue the notorious "kulak lists" that made pariahs of middle peasants) and asked the peasants to wait until the end of the harvest before reconsidering their memberhip in the collectives. Nagy later commented that this speech "left the Party inclined to feel that there was no need for great changes in Party life, leadership, and policy; that actually the old policy could be continued."[10]

These delaying tactics brought to the surface the disagreement between Rákosi and Nagy on the nature of the party-state relationship, a disagreement which was perhaps inevitable in view of the limited minority support that Nagy could muster in the Central Committee and the reluctance of party functionaries to do his bidding in the absence of specific Soviet directives. Nagy was accused of trying to subordinate the party to the state; he later countered this with the charge that prior to 1953 the party had harmfully expropriated the functions of the state organs.[11] Rákosi received an ostensible setback in January, 1954, when following a visit by Nagy, the Kremlin pressed him to cooperate in the implementation of the June resolutions.[12] His May pilgrimage to Moscow to curry favor only elicited new attacks on his obstructionism, and the Third Party Congress, held later that month, endorsed the New Course and reduced the size of the Politburo, without however increasing the proportion of Nagy's supporters. Seeking an alternate power base, Nagy proposed the revival of the Patriotic People's Front, telling the congress that it would mobilize the mass support the party had failed to muster; he then proceeded to staff the fledgling front with his supporters, but the party leadership quickly saw a potential rival in his brain child and successfully stunted its development.[13]

[10] I. Nagy, *On Communism,* p. 283. For Rákosi's and Nagy's speeches, see Royal Institute of International Affairs, *Documents on International Affairs, 1953,* pp. 182–88.

[11] See I. Nagy, *On Communism,* pp. 251–52.

[12] *Ibid.,* p. 281.

[13] See Paul E. Zinner, *Revolution in Hungary* (New York, 1962), p. 169.

Fraught with mishaps and procrastination, the New Course nevertheless achieved some economic reforms by reversing virtually every trend that had characterized the Stalinist period. Membership in collectives fell from a high of 369,200 in 1952 to 230,000 in 1954, a drop of nearly 40 per cent, while the total number of collective farms fell by 14 per cent; productivity continued to be highest on individual farms and lowest on state farms.[14] Investments in heavy industry were 41.1 per cent lower in 1954 than they had been in 1953, and concurrently, investments in light and consumer industries and in agriculture were increased. The decline in the handicraft industries which had led to a serious shortage of essential services in the Rákosi period was halted, and by the end of 1954 there were twice as many artisans as before the New Course.[15] Nagy tried to satisfy consumer demands, not only by augmenting the supply of goods, but also by reducing prices, and as a result of these policies the standard of living did improve, with real wages rising by 18 per cent in 1954.[16] Yet another proposal, to decentralize economic administration and to extend the power of local councils and of the National Assembly, had far-reaching political implications but never progressed beyond the planning stage.

[14] Balassa, *The Hungarian Experience in Economic Planning,* pp. 247, 250; cf. Lajos Fehér, "The Central Problem of Hungary's New Peasant Policy: Alliance with the Middle Peasants," *Társadalmi Szemle,* 9, no. 3 (1954) : 33–56.

[15] Balassa, *The Hungarian Experience in Economic Planning,* p. 36, and Központi Statisztikai Hivatal, *A magyar magánkisipar: 1938–1960* (Budapest, 1961) , p. 9.

[16] Balassa, *The Hungarian Experience in Economic Planning,* p. 37. The author points out that, despite the optimistic projections of the first Five-Year Plan, the standard of living was still lower than it had been in 1938 or 1949; *ibid.,* pp. 228–29.

Although initially some of the old Stalinists such as Révai offered token support for the New Course,[17] the cleavage between party and government remained in evidence; Ernő Gerő continued to run the party's Economic Policy Committee, and he hindered Nagy's efforts at every turn. Inflationary pressures brought charges of extravagance against Nagy, and Gerő and István Friss drew up a report urging harsh deflationary measures, but for once Nagy prevailed; at its October session the Central Committee rejected the proposal and rebuked Rákosi for opposing the New Course.[18] Rákosi was particularly concerned about the impending rehabilitation of the victims of his vast purges, for to have the circumstances of their trials made public would have been politically disastrous. By the end of 1954, however, Nagy succeeded in having most of the purged communists such as Kádár and Losonczy released; other political prisoners remained in custody.[19]

Despite the progress made by the New Course, the contradictory orientations of the rival factions were rapidly leading to an impasse when in November, 1954, Rákosi once again visited Moscow; this time his intriguing bore fruit. The extreme Stalinists, represented by Molotov, and the economic and political reformers, led by Malenkov, were losing ground to the Khrushchev faction, which pressed for a resumption of the rapid expansion of heavy industry.[20] The new, Khrush-

[17] József Révai, "The Struggle for the Achievement of the New Goals," *Társadalmi Szemle,* 7, nos. 10–11 (1953) : 923–36. For a critique of the lingering autarchic tendencies in official circles, see T. Liska and A Máriás, "Optimum Returns and the International Division of Labor," *Közgazdasági Szemle,* 1, no. 1 (1953) : 75–94.

[18] Ferenc A. Váli, *Rift and Revolt in Hungary* (Cambridge, Mass., 1961) , pp. 134–36.

[19] See *ibid.,* chap. 12, *passim.*

[20] See Brzezinski, *The Soviet Bloc,* p. 166.

chevian economic orthodoxy suited Rákosi but was incompatible with Nagy's New Course, and when Nagy arrived at the Kremlin in January, 1955, he found that even Malenkov, shortly to be dismissed, had turned on him. Control finally slipped from Nagy's hands when in March the Central Committee, prodded into action by the opportune appearance of Suslov, formally indicted him for having pursued a policy of "right-wing opportunist deviation." Nagy, who was ill at the time, refused to step down, but an April resolution went even further in charging that his "anti-Marxist, anti-Leninist, anti-Party views . . . form a comprehensive system, an attitude which spread to the various fields of political, economic, and cultural life";[21] the more pliant András Hegedüs replaced him as premier, and in November, 1955, Nagy was expelled from the party.

In literal terms the censure of Nagy was somewhat unjustified, for he had remained loyal to the party, if not to Rákosi, throughout his premiership; only in disgrace did he engage in a fundamental reappraisal of the dogma and veer toward "national communism." It is clear that his fortunes had been directed from Moscow, and observers have pointed out that his rise and fall coincided with Malenkov's career in the Kremlin.[22] Apparently, then, Nagy had been a part of the Soviets' policy of concession while their own leadership problems were being solved, and this was why he had never been allowed to supplant Rákosi entirely.[23] Of greater consequence was Nagy's psychological impact

[21] I. Nagy, *On Communism*, pp. xliii, 103.

[22] See Zinner, *Revolution in Hungary*, p. 147.

[23] Khrushchev allegedly explained his reinstatement of Rákosi by saying, "I have to keep Rákosi in Hungary, because in Hungary the whole structure will collapse if he goes" (quoted in George Mikes, *The Hungarian Revolution* [London, 1957], p. 61).

on the Hungarian people. The New Course had given rise to a wave of overoptimism quickly stifled by his demise, but within the party there materialized an opposition group which abandoned Rákosi's Stalinism for Nagy's more moderate brand of communism, and the masses gradually came to perceive the cracks in the monolith.

Dilemmas of Decompression

The fact that Rákosi's return to dictatorial power did not mean the immediate reimposition of the *status quo ante* can be attributed to both systemic and internal causes. The new orthodoxy introduced by Khrushchev was a blend of economic neo-Stalinism, modest political relaxation and decentralization, and "peaceful coexistence." Of these components, only the first suited the Hungarian party chief, for the other two potentially weakened him by allowing for a degree of particularistic revisionism. The Soviet reconciliation with Tito was particularly irksome to Rákosi, and the former paid him back in kind by denouncing him bitterly for having his hands "soaked in blood."[24] In the event, Rákosi's main (and no doubt reluctant) contribution to the *détente* was the transfer of Cardinal Mindszenty from prison to house arrest in July, 1955, and the subsequent release of Archbishop Grősz and a number of priests. He responded to the June Belgrade declaration with a speech blaming the already imprisoned AVH chief, Gábor Péter, for the anti-Tito hate campaign of years past.

In the economic sphere, investments and production

[24] Royal Institute of International Affairs, *Documents on International Affairs, 1955* (London, 1958), p. 271.

goals for heavy industry were stepped up at the expense of the more consumer-oriented industries, while renewed efforts at collectivization reversed the flow of peasants leaving the collectives. In the political sphere, on the other hand, Rákosi's freedom of action was now circumscribed by the legatees of the New Course. Within the party there were several forces aligned against Rákosi's reassertion of absolute power: the rehabilitated communists whom he had purged (mostly homebred like Kádár, Losonczy, Donáth), those lower functionaries who had sympathized with the New Course while doing Rákosi's bidding, and the increasingly restive intellectual establishment. Thus Rákosi's comeback was qualified both by the new attitude in the Kremlin and by the erosion of party unity at home.

The progressive disaffection within party circles and the more gradual articulation of popular discontent have been termed respectively the élite process and the mass process in the genesis of the 1956 revolution.[25] In the first process the consolidation of the revisionist faction was made possible by systemic developments that ruled out show trials and indiscriminate purges; indeed, the AVH proved increasingly reluctant to implement Rákosi's political machinations. The leading force in this intraparty revisionism was Imre Nagy, although it must be emphasized that his role was intellectual and ideological and only marginally power-seeking or conspiratorial. Nagy had prepared a brief to justify his actions before the Central Committee, but after his expulsion he elaborated this into a bitter condemnation of the party orthodoxy and an indirect criticism of Soviet hegemony. Nagy's critique, though less secular or analytical than the later writings of Leszek Kola-

[25] See Kecskeméti, *The Unexpected Revolution, passim.*

kowski in Poland, provided tangible evidence of the spread of the "national communism" concept—the very Titoist infection that Stalin had feared and abhorred. Going far beyond the scope of the June resolutions, which had been concerned primarily with economic matters, the critique blamed Stalin for sanctioning Rákosi's excesses and argued that Titoism could not be regarded as a deviation from Marxism-Leninism. Bemoaning the sorry state of the party, Nagy called for its moral and political regeneration and denounced Rákosi's "Führerism":

As a result of the degeneration of power, individuals whose actions went counter to the morals of socialist society and to existing laws acquired positions in important fields of public life. It is not compatible to have in positions of leadership the directors and organizers of mass trials, those responsible for torturing and killing innocent men, organizers of international provocations, and economic saboteurs or squanderers of public property who, through the abuse of power, either have committed serious acts against the people or are forcing others to commit these acts.[26]

He warned that public opinion was condemning both the party and the government and would reject these unless rapid action was taken to pacify it. Nagy's writings were also distinguished by a nationalistic quality that had been notably absent from the statements of the orthodox leadership: he revived Kossuth's vision of "close cooperation with neighbouring peoples within the framework of free and independent nations," accused those in power of accepting "dependence, subordination, humiliating slavery"—a scarcely veiled al-

[26] I. Nagy, *On Communism*, pp. 13, 55.

lusion to the Soviet Union—and urged that Hungary remain neutral in the competition between "power groups."[27]

The fact that Nagy was not immediately liquidated for his heresy was due partly to the concurrent reconciliation between Moscow and Belgrade, and partly to the fact that his extreme thesis did not circulate beyond a close circle of friends. The shifts in ideological orthodoxy, however, had the effect of unsettling the hitherto decidedly sycophantic intellectual etablishment.

Numerically small, culturally of limited significance, and composed of a few older populists (such as the outstanding poet Gyula Illyés) and some younger writers, this official intelligentsia had been motivated by opportunism as well as idealism in faithfully endorsing the excesses of Stalinism.[28] The revelations and vacillations of the New Course occasioned a *crise de conscience* which led them to increasingly radical forms of revisionism. Rákosi's attempts to stifle this dissent by purging the staffs of *Szabad Nép* (the party daily) and *Irodalmi Ujság* (the organ of the Writers' Union) elicited in October, 1955, the "Writers' Memorandum," an almost seditious document signed by more than fifty writers. Deploring censorship, the banning of certain noncommunist works, and the recent purges, the memorandum found the "despotic, anti-democratic methods of leadership in the cultural field more and more intolerable."[29] Rákosi retaliated with new cen-

[27] *Ibid.*, pp. 24, 33–34.

[28] The regime would subsequently argue that 70 per cent of the intelligentsia had been a product of the precommunist period and therefore was tainted with bourgeois values; *Népszava*, June 8, 1958, cited in Brzezinski, *The Soviet Bloc*, p. 219.

[29] *The Truth About the Nagy Affair* (London, 1959), pp. 129–30.

sures and expulsions, but in retrospect this may well have been a critical miscalculation, for it was his harsh treatment of Nagy and the writers that caused the public to take note of their admittedly equivocal hostility to the party and to follow their battle with growing excitement and enthusiasm.

The position of the revisionists was immeasurably strengthened by Khrushchev's anti-Stalin speech at the Twentieth Party Congress in February, 1956. Rákosi, the most rabidly Stalinist of all satellite leaders, felt particularly threatened since his very existence was a denial of the new orthodoxy of collective leadership. The dissolution of the Cominform in April and the Soviet-Yugoslav declaration of friendship and cooperation in June isolated him even further. Emboldened, the writers renewed their attacks on Rákosi and through the *Irodalmi Ujság* acquired for the first time a nation-wide audience and prestige; wrote the old Muscovite Gyula Háy, "The cult of personality has contaminated all of our literature."[30] The writers' demands for cultural freedom and for a realistic appraisal of the plight of the masses pointed to a painful but definite emancipation from the bonds of ideology, even though in practical terms they aimed no further than the replacement of Rákosi by Nagy.

The dearth of channels for the articulation of popular demands at first limited revisionism to these intra-élite debates, and although the writers looked in particular to the industrial workers for support, the latter were intensely suspicious of any appeals originating in the establishment and remained uninvolved.[31] The

---

[30] *Irodalmi Ujság,* May 5, 1956, cited in Kecskeméti. *The Unexpected Revolution,* p. 71. An account of the revisionist intelligentsia's activities is given in Tamás Aczél and Tibor Méray, *The Revolt of the Mind* (New York and London, 1960).

[31] Kecskeméti, *The Unexpected Revolution,* p. 79.

main response came instead from the ranks of the students. The policy of the Rákosi regime in higher education had been to increase the proportion of working-class and peasant students at the expense of the kulak class and "class enemies," but the heavy-handed indoctrination that characterized the educational process could not prevent the students from perceiving the sharp contrast between theory and reality; this perception in turn produced a cynicism that was only partially qualified by a carryover of religious faith.[32] A catalyst for bringing together students and party and extraparty intellectuals was provided by the Petőfi Circle, an outgrowth of the DISZ sanctioned by the party in March, 1956, as a relatively harmless escape valve. Instead, the group became a forum for dissent which was copied in most provincial cities, and by July Gerő was referring to it as the "second leading center" in the country, in other words a rival to the party.[33] Apparently innocuous discussions turned increasingly into mass protest meetings. In June more than a thousand people heard György Lukács, the prominent Marxist philosopher and literary critic, announce the bankruptcy of Marxism in Hungary.[34] The Poznań riots and other developments in Poland only encouraged the dissenters.

The atmosphere created by the new freedom of expression which intellectuals and students were arrogating to themselves could not be tolerated by Rákosi, and

[32] See Elinor Murray, "Higher Education in Communist Hungary, 1948–1956," *The American Slavic and East European Review,* 19, no. 3 (1960) : 395–413.

[33] Zinner, *Revolution in Hungary,* p. 195; cf. William E. Griffith, "The Petőfi Circle: Forum for Ferment in the Hungarian Thaw," *Hungarian Quarterly,* 2, no. 1 (1962) : 142–65.

[34] On Lukács' career, see Morris Watnick, "Relativism and Class Consciousness: Georg Lukács," in *Revisionism,* ed. Leopold Labedz (New York, 1962) , pp. 142–65.

on June 30 the Central Committee adopted a resolution condemning the "anti-Party manifestations" in the Petőfi Circle, noting that certain speakers had gone as far as "to deny the leading role of the Party of the working class, and advocated bourgeois and counter-revolutionary views," and alleging that the open opposition had been organized by a faction around Imre Nagy.[35] Two writers, Tibor Déry and Tibor Tárdos, were expelled from the party, but this was a mild reaction indeed to a debate in which the audience "shouted down and disturbed the speeches which presented the correct Party attitude [yet] enthusiastically applauded every attack on the Party and the People's Democracy."[36] Then on July 16 Rákosi presented to the Politburo a plan to arrest the top four hundred troublemakers, including Nagy, to dissolve the Writers' Union and the Petőfi Circle, to suspend publication of *Irodalmi Ujság,* and to prepare a trial of the antiparty conspirators. Clearly he regretted earlier concessions such as the rehabilitation of Rajk in March and the more recent release of thousands of political internees.

This return to Stalinism was thwarted by the appearance on July 17 of Anastas Mikoyan, who unceremoniously ordered the replacement of Rákosi by Ernő Gerő as first secretary, a change reflecting Moscow's view that Rákosi was too unpopular both in Hungary and with Tito to warrant further tenure, while Nagy was becoming too nationalistic to represent an acceptable alternative.[37] A Stalinist at heart, Gerő set out to

[35] Paul E. Zinner, ed., *National Communism and Popular Revolt in Eastern Europe* (New York, 1956), p. 329.

[36] *Ibid.,* p. 334.

[37] Tito recapitulated after the revolution:

When increasingly strong dissatisfaction began to rise to the surface in the ranks of the Hungarian Communists themselves, and when they demanded that Rákosi should go, the Soviet

gain time by steering a middle course between "sectarianism" and "right-wing opportunism." He promised to improve economic management and to maintain "socialist legality" and reshuffled the Central Committee, bringing in some of Rákosi's victims, such as János Kádár; he also expelled from the party the most hated member of the Rákosi quadrumvirate, former Minister of Defense Mihály Farkas. A new Central Committee resolution dealing with party policy toward the intelligentsia acknowledged several shortcomings, such as the excessive teaching of party history, and promised a variety of reforms, both material and cultural, including the discontinuance of cadre materials (i.e., police files) on intellectuals.[38]

The choice of the intrinsically doctrinaire Gerő was an unhappy one, for what have been termed the classical symptoms of a prerevolutionary period were already in evidence: the alienation of the intellectuals, disorganization within the ruling circles, and widespread social unrest. At the annual general meeting of the Writers' Union on September 17, complete freedom for writers and punishment for their erstwhile censors were demanded by the speakers. The concurrent election by secret ballot of the new executive committee saw the defeat of all party candidates.[39] The totality of party control had been broken. The leading

---

leaders realized that it was impossible to continue in this way and agreed that he should be removed. But they committed a mistake by not also allowing the removal of Gerő and other Rákosi followers, who had compromised themselves in the eyes of the people. They made it a condition that Rákosi would go only if Gerő remained. And this was a mistake, because Gerő differed in no way from Rákosi. He pursued the same kind of policy and was to blame as much as Rákosi was. *Ibid.,* p. 524.

[38] *Ibid,* p. 381.

[39] *Ibid.,* p. 383.

role in this process of disintegration gradually passed from the revisionists to the students and other extra-party elements, and attempts by the apparat to retain the direction of liberalization only strengthened the latter. On September 28 the Central Council of Trade-Unions adopted a resolution demanding more autonomy and welfare for workers. At the beginning of October the final act in the history of the Rajk purge took place. Rajk's supporters and many others who sensed the regime's vulnerability had long agitated for ceremonial rehabilitation, and Gerő, who was engaged in the difficult task of winning Tito's endorsement, decided to accede to their requests. The macabre ceremony that took place in Budapest on October 6, when with great pomp Rajk was reinterred, provided the occasion for an unprecedented mass demonstration against not only the Rákosi clique but also the incumbent leadership. A further concession was the reinstatement of Imre Nagy on October 13, although the Politburo pointedly reminded revisionists that he had indeed "committed political mistakes."[40]

While Gerő visited Belgrade to reach an eleventh-hour accommodation with Tito, events in Hungary indicated that instead of appeasing the public, the denouement of the Rajk affair had only whetted its appetite, and news of the successful stand taken by Gomulka and the Poles against Soviet interference was received with widespread enthusiasm. University students throughout the country stepped up their agitation for everything from a reduction in compulsory Marxism-Leninism courses to better dormitories. The reactivated Petőfi Circle adopted a resolution listing ten demands; these included the reinstatement of Imre Nagy to the government, revision of the second Five-

[40] See *ibid.*, pp. 386–89.

Year Plan, the expulsion of Rákosi from the party, the public trial of Farkas, the publication of foreign trade agreements, including those covering the Soviet exploitation of Hungarian uranium, and freedom of expression in literature.[41] The idea of student manifestoes spread like wildfire, and a new independent student organization came into being at Szeged on October 16. It was at the Technical University in Budapest that the most crucial demand was finally voiced: the call for the evacuation of Soviet troops. On October 23, the morning after that last demand, *Szabad Nép* noted in an editorial that the students were in the vast majority not "bourgeois reactionaries" but "firm believers in socialism" and that they had previously been repressed and were now giving proof of "serious political maturity"; after a rather timid warning against counterrevolutionary manifestations the editorial closed with a few lines from a poem by Endre Ady which spoke of a happy transformation.

The Revolt of the Masses

The mass process, which became manifest only in the few days preceding the outbreak of violence, illustrated the phenomenon of decompression that de Tocqueville had described more than a century earlier when he observed that the evils which are endured with patience as long as they are inevitable seem intolerable as soon as hope can be entertained of escaping them. The myth of the party as a monolithic body with an unimpeachable ideology had been destroyed by the rise of revisionism, and the consequent division in the élite proved to be the major catalytic factor in the collapse of the

41 *Ibid.*, pp. 391–92.

entire system. The momentary alliance between previously irreconcilable elements—the alienated masses and the increasingly secular revisionist intelligentsia—and the concurrent atrophy or passivity of the system's regulative organs left the orthodox leadership without an adequate basis of support at the critical moment of open revolt.

Few historical events have received as thorough a chronological and analytical treatment as the Hungarian revolution of 1956; in the present context our consideration will be limited to certain salient social, political, and systemic aspects of its development.[42]

In a period of thirteen days the revolution passed through several distinct phases. The initial phase ended with the final demise of the Gerő group and Imre Nagy's accession to power. The second phase saw the evolution of the Nagy government under popular pressure toward a multiparty coalition. The third phase began with the declaration of Hungary's neutrality and ended with the forcible removal of the revolutionary regime on November 4. In less than two weeks the gamut had been run from totalitarianism to popular democracy and back to totalitarianism, but in the interval there had been created in the Communist bloc a breach which placed the Western Powers as well as the Soviet Union in a unique dilemma.

Although it has been alleged that Gerő was planning to provoke a minor insurrection in order to purge his opponents,[43] the momentum of dissent caught him unprepared. On his return from Belgrade on October

[42] In addition to the studies cited in this chapter, see the compilation of I. L. Halász de Béky, *A Bibliography of the Hungarian Revolution, 1956* (Toronto, 1963).

[43] See Váli, *Rift and Revolt in Hungary*, p. 273, and Zinner, *Revolution in Hungary*, p. 254.

114

23, he agreed to the appointment of Nagy as figurehead-premier, but at the same time another Politburo member, György Marosán, quietly called for Soviet assistance. A peaceful demonstration of students that evening, intended as a gesture of sympathy for the Poles, became inflamed by the broadcast of a declaration by Gerő, in which the latter qualified the demonstrators as enemies of the people who were undermining the power of the working class and whose criticisms of the Soviet military presence and of exploitative trade agreements did not contain a grain of truth.[44] Gerő's harsh words exacerbated an already oversensitive public opinion, and while he spoke the demonstrators' aggressiveness increased. One group set about toppling a huge statue of Stalin; others gathered before the Parliament, the *Szabad Nép* offices, and the central studio of Radio Budapest. A key aspect of modern totalitarianism is control of the airwaves, and the demonstrators knew this when they demanded that their manifesto be broadcast. Gerő's hard line was translated into action when, late in the evening of October 23, the panicky AVH detachment assigned to guard the radio building fired the first shots into the crowd below; Hungarian army units dispatched to the scene either remained passive or joined the insurgents, making it evident that the regime's effective support had dwindled to the deeply implicated secret police and the Soviet armored troops who arrived the following morning. The bloodiest encounter occurred at midday on October 25 in front of the Parliament; there a group of demonstrators had been waiting for Nagy and fraternizing with the increasingly demoralized Russians

[44] Zinner, *National Communism*, pp. 402–7. Regarding the uranium mines, see J. Stomfay-Stiltz, "Der Ungarische Uranbergbau," *Osteuropa,* 7, no. 3 (1957) : 203–6.

when AVH agents opened fire on the crowd and precipitated a pitched battle.

By that time even the Kremlin had come to appreciate the untenable position of the Gerő regime, for on the 24th Suslov and Mikoyan had been dispatched to Budapest to appraise the situation. Gerő was replaced by János Kádár as first secretary, and both the latter and Nagy issued conciliatory statements acknowledging the "honest aims" of the demonstrators and promising wide-ranging reforms and negotiations toward the withdrawal of Soviet forces stationed in Hungary.[45] Meanwhile revolutionary councils and committees had materialized in factories and throughout the provinces and they began to send a barrage of demands to the capital. These pressures led to a major reorganization of the government on October 27; for the first time since 1948 it included representatives of other parties such as the Smallholder Zoltán Tildy and the Peasant Party member Ferenc Erdei. Still, the majority in the government were communists, primarily revisionists like Kádár and Lukács.

Thus the first phase of the revolution ended. Through the obduracy of Gerő, events had run a course which was far from parallel to developments in Poland, for the bloodshed sparked a nationalistic, revolutionary spirit of solidarity among Hungarians that precluded any voluntary return either to Soviet tutelage or to purely communist rule. In the event, the cleavage between Nagy and the revisionists on the one hand and the vast majority of revolutionary groups on the other was too great to allow the new government any degree of permanence.

While political freedom was one of the insurgents'

---

[45] Zinner, *National Communism,* pp. 415–18.

chief aims, they were most adamant on the question of Soviet withdrawal, and a vicious circle ensued. Moscow was willing to tolerate a reformist regime as long as the supremacy of the Communist Party was maintained —necessarily by the presence of Soviet armed force. The revolutionaries rejected any government that did not promise immediate withdrawal. Clearly Nagy did not have Moscow's mandate to make this promise, although he frequently reiterated that negotiations with the Soviet Union were in progress. Other factors contributed to Nagy's weakness. A somewhat indecisive man, he lacked the charismatic quality that might have rallied support for a "national communist" solution. Nor was he helped at this stage by such an extraneous critic as Radio Free Europe, which in the early days of the revolution saw in his appointment a Trojan-horse tactic.[46] In broadcasting the program of his new government on October 28, Nagy conceded that the uprising was no counterrevolution and announced that agreement had been reached for a Russian military withdrawal from Budapest.[47] The revolutionary councils retained the initiative, however, by demanding general and free elections and the complete evacuation of Soviet forces.

Apparently Moscow was still hesitant, for Khrushchev later indicated that the Soviet leadership had been divided on the wisdom of intervention.[48] A likely division might have ranged from the Stalinist diehards— Molotov, Suslov, and Lazar Kaganovich—through the

[46] Méray, *Thirteen Days that Shook the Kremlin,* p. 140; cf. Miklós Molnár and Lázló Nagy, *Imre Nagy: Réformateur ou révolutionnaire?* (Geneva, 1959) .

[47] Zinner, *National Communism,* pp. 428–32.

[48] Zinner, *Revolution in Hungary,* p. 320; cf. Giuseppe Boffa, *Inside the Khrushchev Era* (New York, 1959) , p. 105.

centrist Khrushchev to the moderate Mikoyan. The liberals had won out over the crisis in Poland and had been proved correct by the preservation of the communist system under Gomulka, but Hungary was qualitatively a very different test case. Mikoyan and Suslov paid a second visit to Budapest on October 27 and yet another on the 31st. In the interval, on October 30, the Soviet government issued a declaration on "Principles of Development and Further Strengthening of Friendship and Cooperation Between the Soviet Union and Other Socialist States."[49] It upheld peaceful coexistence on the basis "of complete equality, of respect for territorial integrity, state independence and sovereignty, and of non-interference in one another's internal affairs," but warned against foreign and domestic reactionary forces.

Despite the ostensible willingness of Mikoyan to negotiate, the Soviet leadership must have decided to intervene when on October 30 Nagy acceded to popular pressure and proclaimed the restoration of the multiparty system and of a representative coalition government which now also included the Social Democrats.[50] Two days later, alarmed at new Soviet troop movements and overwhelmed by nationwide demands, Nagy took the crucial step of announcing Hungary's neutrality and withdrawal from the Warsaw Pact; he declared that "today our people are as united in this decision as perhaps never before in their history" and rested his case with the United Nations.[51] Kádár announced his party's endorsement of the decision, then surreptitiously left the capital in the company of other ranking communists.

[49] Zinner, *National Communism*, pp. 487–89.
[50] *Ibid.*, p. 449.
[51] *Ibid.*, pp. 462–64.

118

In retrospect, subsequent developments were almost anticlimactic. The government underwent a final reorganization on November 3, with wider representation being given to noncommunists in the four-party coalition. Despite the continuing influx of Soviet troops, Moscow maintained a conciliatory facade and agreed to negotiate on the military aspects of Nagy's demands. On the night of November 3 a Hungarian delegation, having gone in good faith to the Russian headquarters outside Budapest, was summarily arrested by the head of the Soviet security police, General Serov. Concurrently a massive attack was launched on all points of resistance, and the following morning a broadcast originating from Russian territory announced the formation by Kádár and Ferenc Münnich of a "Hungarian Revolutionary Worker-Peasant government" which repudiated the popular nature of the revolution and called upon the Soviet army to smash the "sinister forces of reaction."[52] The revolution had run its course.

A social analysis of the revolutionary forces shows a remarkably wide distribution across traditional class lines, although recent Hungarian attempts at historical revisionism stress the role of underground clerical and veterans' organizations and *Lumpenproletariat* elements, and the loyalty of the genuine working classes.[53] In fact, although the sources of revolutionary impetus changed with the succeeding phases, the profoundly nationalistic nature of the uprising struck a responsive chord in all socioeconomic groups. One survey showed that the proportion of active (i.e., fighting) revolu-

[52] *Ibid.*, pp. 473–78.

[53] János Molnár, *Ellenforradalom Magyarországon 1956-ban* (Budapest, 1967), pp. 57–58. This recent study is notable for occasional candid glimpses into the revolution which are introduced under the guise of debunking "bourgeois" accounts of that event. Cf. Zinner, *Revolution in Hungary*, p. 272.

tionaries among professionals was 14 per cent, among white-collar workers 2 per cent, among industrial workers 13 per cent, among peasants 6 per cent, and among students and others 20 per cent.[54] Other members of these groups engaged in nonviolent supporting activities; the intelligentsia had the lowest and the white-collar class the highest proportion of ostensibly inactive individuals. In the initial prerevolutionary stage the revisionists acted as the vanguard, while the first phase of the revolution saw students and young people take the most active role; the old dispossessed classes were particularly reluctant to become involved at first, partly because of distrust and partly because they recognized that their role might be misconstrued. The formation of workers' councils and revolutionary committees, and of semi-autonomous insurgent units such as that led by József Dudás, brought into play a wider cross-section of society ranging from opportunistic adventurers to political prisoners just released by the revolutionaries. Since the locus of revolutionary activity was primarily Budapest and other urban areas, the peasants played a relatively passive role, but they participated in the neutralization of the more intransigent rural apparatchiks and fulfilled their traditional function of voluntarily supplying food for the urban combatants. Finally, with the reactivation of the old Independence Front parties, the postwar noncommunist political élite—notably Béla Kovács and the Social Democrat Anna Kéthly—returned to the fray.

Of the prerevolutionary regulative organs only the AVH survived the outbreak of rebellion, its loyalty being dictated by its operations on behalf of the despised Rákosi regime; the secret police were fully justi-

---

[54] Kecskeméti, *The Unexpected Revolution*, pp. 109–10.

fied in fearing the wrath of the masses, for, in the event, few survived popular identification. As we noted previously, the military subsystem had been purged of apparently disloyal elements, but many of these were released if not reinstated in the months preceding the revolution, and the officer corps as a whole had sympathized with the revisionists; the rank and file felt even less compunction about joining the rebels.[55] Officers such as Béla Király and Pál Maléter, the latter acquiring fame as the defender of the Kilián barracks, played a dominant role in the attempts to fuse the various military units and revolutionary groups into a National Guard. Király became the military commander of Budapest, while Maléter acted as minister of defense in the last Nagy government, only to be arrested by Serov with the other members of the November 3 delegation. The regular police proved equally susceptible to the call of revolution. Budapest's chief of police, Sándor Kopácsi, at first ordered his men to be passive, then collaborated fully with the new regimes. None of the Rákosi era's mobilizing institutions survived decompression: students and young people formed new organizations, and the old Trade Union Council was dissolved to make way for new, independent unions, although a nationwide strike remained in force until the last day of the uprising.

The disintegration of Stalinist rule allowed a relatively heterogeneous belief system to surface once again. Although up to October 23 the revisionists remained in the vanguard of the reform movement by virtue of their access to the media, thereafter the immense disil-

[55] An exceptional clash occurred at Magyaróvár on October 26, when the élite Frontier Guards killed eighty demonstrators; see Béla Király, "Hungary's Army: Its Part in the Revolt," *East Europe,* 7, no. 6 (1958) : 3–15.

lusionment of the working classes and the momentum of decompression relegated them to a supporting role, and, to the extent that Nagy was one of them, he too performed as follower rather than leader in this essentially leaderless revolution. The dominant value became national independence; the dominant sentiment, patriotism. Nationalism subsumed freedom from Soviet suzerainty, and the masses in their astuteness or naïveté rejected the road of national communism. The emergence of the old "middle-class" values was not, however, an entirely retrogressive and undifferentiated phenomenon. The reappearance of noncommunist parties occurred in response to a popular consensus favoring a multiparty system, and the core of these parties necessarily consisted of the remnants of their postwar élites, but there is little indication that a return to a semifeudal capitalistic system was considered desirable or imminent. Even an adamantine and conservative prelate like Cardinal Mindszenty refrained from advocating such a step. Although in his speech of November 3 he stopped short of unequivocally endorsing the Nagy government and urged the formation of a Christian Democratic Party, Mindszenty anticipated a liberal democratic system based on private property only to the extent that it would be consistent with social needs.[56]

The programmatic contribution of the new parties was aborted by the Soviet occupation, but by November 3 there appeared the outlines of a pluralistic political system encompassing common as well as conflicting interests.[57] At that time not all these interests were

[56] Melvin J. Lasky, ed., *The Hungarian Revolution: A White Book* (New York, 1957), p. 216.

[57] See László Révész, "Das Ungarische Oktober-Programm," *Der Europäische Osten,* 11 (1968) : 675–77.

represented by political parties. The most urgent pressures toward political reform and Hungarian neutrality had come from provincial revolutionary committees, notably the Transdanubian Council at Győr, and from groups such as that led by Dudás, who in direct competition with the Nagy regime created a short-lived National Committee and was momentarily arrested on Nagy's orders. The workers' councils that materialized in factories and other industrial concerns did not manifest a distinctive ideology apart from favoring the nationalistic goals of the revolution and generally opposing any return to an unqualified capitalistic system.[58] Various Catholic groupings had also coalesced by November 3, evidently attracting the more clerical and traditionalistic elements, and conceivably they were the harbingers of a powerful Christian Democratic Party, while old populists such as Áron Tamási, László Németh, and István Bibó formed the core of the Petőfi (National Peasant) Party. This proliferation of political movements was indicative of the tenuous link that the original revisionists had had with the masses, a fact borne out also by the desperate attempts of the rump Communist Party to liberalize and halt the rapid erosion of its clientele.

The over-all ideology of the revolution, dominated though it was by the goal of national independence, embodied fairly consistent and generalized demands for political and economic reform,[59] and was articulated

[58] See Oskar Anweiler, "Die Räte in der Ungarischen Revolution, 1956," *Osteuropa,* 8, no. 6 (1958) : 393–400. According to the party line, most of the genuine working class stood by, weaponless and impotent, while extreme right-wing elements usurped power in their name; J. Molnár, *Ellenforradalom,* pp. 64ff.

[59] See Edmund O. Stillman, *Ideology of the Revolution* (New York, 1957).

in its most comprehensive form by the populist scholar István Bibó, a minister of state in the last Nagy government. Briefly, Bibó urged that Hungary take the "third road" lying between the capitalist and communist archtypes, a road which would synthesize the more positive and relevant aspects of socialism and capitalism into a mixed economy, allow the development of a multiparty system consistent with the preservation of socialist achievements, and turn Hungary into a neutral actor in the international system.[60] This essentially national, neutralist, non-Marxist, yet progressive ideology probably would have predominated in the value system of an independent postrevolutionary Hungary.

Disintegration and Reintegration

The party line that subsequently provided the official interpretation of the revolution maintained that the "counterrevolution was a revolt against socialism aiming ultimately at the overthrow of the people's power, a revolt arising from sectarian errors and misdeeds, encouraged and assisted by imperialism, organized by indigenous reactionaries, and facilitated by revisionism."[61] In fact, Kádár's Revolutionary Worker-

[60] István Bibó, *Harmadik Ut* (London, 1960); cf. François Fejtő, "Hungarian Communism," in *Communism in Europe,* ed. William E. Griffith, 2 vols. (Cambridge, Mass., 1964), 1: 188–90, and Gyula Borbándi, "István Bibó: Hungary's Political Philosopher," *East Europe,* 13, no. 10 (1964) : 2–7.

[61] J. Molnár, *Ellenforradalom,* p. 240. The same source concedes that the few returning *émigrés* had exerted a negligible influence; *ibid.,* p. 167. Cf. *The Counter-revolutionary Forces in the October Events in Hungary* (Budapest, 1957), and *The Counter-revolutionary Conspiracy of Imre Nagy and His Accomplices* (Budapest, 1958).

Peasant government returned to symbolize a power held by the Soviet occupation forces, which had for the second time in twenty years taken administrative charge of Hungary. Workers' councils had supplanted the defunct Nagy government as negotiators on the side of the revolution, and there prevailed for a time the paradox of a general strike in protest against the reimposition of a dictatorship of the proletariat.[62] Mass deportations and executions prompted the councils to call off the general strike, but demonstrations continued and the Russians' kidnapping of Nagy upon his departure from the Yugoslav Embassy on November 23 suggested that he was still feared as a potential rallying point. The initial proclamations of the Kádár group included promises of economic reforms and eventual Soviet evacuation, and Kádár even undertook negotiations to include noncommunists in an ostensibly coalition government, but clearly the gap between Bibó's "third road" and the course acceptable to the Soviet Union was too great.[63] On December 9, in order to forestall a forty-eight-hour protest strike, Kádár proclaimed martial law and dissolved all workers' councils above the factory level.

Concurrently, the Provisional Central Committee of the renamed Hungarian Socialist Workers' Party released a manifesto which foreshadowed Kádár's subsequent centrist line.[64] By accusing both the Rákosi-Gerő sectarians and the Nagy group of deviating from genuine Marxism-Leninism, the manifesto postulated an *ex post facto* ideological identity between the new party and the 1953–54 New Course. In the short run

[62] See Hannah Arendt, *Die ungarische Revolution und der totalitäre Imperialismus* (Munich, 1958), p. 154.

[63] Váli, *Rift and Revolt in Hungary*, p. 387.

[64] See Fejtő, "Hungarian Communism," pp. 219ff.

his ploy failed to seduce the remaining revolutionary elite, and passive resistance continued. A conference in Budapest on January 4, 1957, brought together Khrushchev and Malenkov and their hard-line supporters from Bulgaria, Czechoslovakia, and Rumania in a display of support for Kádár. The latter thereafter changed tack; he ordered the arrest of several writers, dissolved the Writers' Union, and delivered the verdict that the revolution had indeed been a counterrevolutionary phenomenon.[65] Addressing a restive assembly of Hungarian miners in April, 1958, Khrushchev voiced the ultimate epitaph over that event: "Your demonstration is in vain. You have to swallow the fact: What is to be will be."[66]

The momentum of the revolution did not allow the other socialist states to influence events in Hungary directly, but their responses indicated a degree of ideological ambivalence. East Germany, Czechoslovakia, and Rumania followed Moscow's line from the start and did not hesitate to give their official support to the Kádár regime; the solidarity of the last two was bolstered by the prorevolutionary enthusiasm of their Magyar minorities. Poland, in the midst of a less violent transitional phase, reacted more positively; the Polish press reported the developments in Hungary with remarkable objectivity, and the traditional ties between the two nations added to the sympathy felt by the Poles. Gomulka, however, could ill afford to antagonize the Soviet Union and thereby lose what he had gained for Poland, and, accordingly, official opinion bowed to the Kremlin and condemned the "forces of reaction pushing Hungary towards disaster."[67]

[65] *Népszabadság*, February 12, 1957.
[66] *Ibid.*, April 10, 1958.
[67] Zinner, *National Communism*, p. 282.

Yugoslavia, like Poland, had looked favorably on the revolution as long as its aim was independence under, not from, communism. Tito declared at Pula on November 11 that "viewing current developments in Hungary from the perspective of socialism or counter-revolution, we must defend Kádár's present Government, we must help."[68] The diplomatic insult inherent in Nagy's kidnapping evoked mild protests, and these, together with vocal support for the workers' councils and lingering doubts about the Russian verdict of counterrevolution, contributed to strained relations between the Soviet Union and Yugoslavia. The Russians suspected that Tito had actively encouraged Nagy, and admittedly it would have pleased Tito to see Nagy establish a national communist regime, but he probably reasoned that even Kádár was preferable to a neutral and liberal democratic Hungary, and that in the long battle against Stalinism even this was a minor victory.

As for the Chinese People's Republic, its reactions to the revolution followed a haphazard course. Its initial response, when Nagy still appeared to be another Gomulka, was that the Soviet Union was guilty of great-nation chauvinism; later the Chinese claimed that they had put pressure on a wavering Soviet government to step in and crush the revolution.[69] Premier

[68] *Ibid.,* p. 516; cf. Duka Julius, "Hungary After Its Tragedy," *Review of International Affairs* (Belgrade), 7, no. 161 (1956) : 9,

[69] Recalled the Peking *People's Daily* on September 5, 1963: "At the critical moment, when the Hungarian counterrevolutionaries had occupied Budapest, for a time [the Soviet leaders] intended to adopt a policy of capitulation and abandon Socialist Hungary. . . . We insisted on the taking of all necessary measures to smash the counterrevolutionaries." Cf. Edward Crankshaw, *The New Cold War: Moscow vs. Peking* (London, 1963), pp. 53–55.

Chou En-lai visited Budapest in January to give his blessing to the Kádár regime, although the resulting communiqué did make passing reference to the legitimate discontent of the masses.[70]

Evidently none of the communist regimes was unhappy to see Hungary return to the fold, but this is not to say that the repercussions of the affair had not penetrated deeply; as Djilas observed, "the wound which the Hungarian Revolution inflicted on Communism can never be completely healed."[71]

Since the period covered by this chapter was most notable for disintegrative tendencies within the system, developments in the sphere of economic cooperation have been left for later consideration. On the politico-military front, an institutional innovation had been the creation of the Warsaw Pact "Of Friendship, Cooperation, and Mutual Aid."[72] Signed on May 14, 1955, the day before the Austrian State Treaty presumably would have eliminated the need for Soviet troops to guard lines of communication through Hungary, the agreement established a joint military command and a body for political consultation. Article 5 provided for mutual defense and implicitly legalized the stationing of Soviet troops on the territories of the signatories. The pact represented a step toward military integration under the effective guidance of a Soviet commanding officer, although the Hungarian revolution cast some doubt on the reliability of its non-Soviet components. (The Gerő regime subsequently claimed that it was requesting Russian assistance in accordance with the terms of the Warsaw Treaty, but legally this was

[70] See Fejtő, "Hungarian Communism," pp. 226–27.

[71] Quoted in Lasky, *The Hungarian Revolution*, p. 270.

[72] McNeal, *International Relations Among Communists*, pp. 80–83.

a spurious excuse since there was no apparent threat to Hungary's territorial integrity.)[73] At the end of 1955 Hungary was admitted to the United Nations under an East-West package deal, but it was not until 1962 that the credentials of the Kádár regime's delegation were accepted. In the interim the U.N.'s consideration of the Soviet invasion—from the first Security Council meeting to the report of the special committee and subsequent reappraisals by a special representative on Hungary—proved to be an exercise in futility because of the deliberately passive posture of the United States.[74]

In sum, the Hungarian revolution demonstrated the failure of the Stalinist period's integrative efforts to overcome nationalistic forces and to implant a new and all-encompassing belief system in Eastern Europe. However, both the thaw and the revolution saw the development of a degree of pluralism and revisionism which proved irreversible, despite the use of force in Hungary. While the fortunes of the East Europeans were still ultimately determined by decisions made in Moscow—continuous supervision and direction prevailed even during the revolution—a process of consultation which allowed for differences in local conditions replaced the procrustean tactics of the period of intensive socialization.

[73] Zinner, *National Communism,* p. 409; cf. Ferenc A. Váli, *The Hungarian Revolution and International Law* (New York, 1959), Joseph A. Szikszoy, *The Legal Aspects of the Hungarian Question* (Geneva, 1963), and International Commission of Jurists, *Report on the Hungarian Situation and the Rule of Law,* 3 vols. (The Hague, 1957–58).

[74] See United Nations, General Assembly, *Official Records,* 11th Sess., Suppl. 18 (A/3592), *Report of the Special Committee on the Problem of Hungary* (New York, 1957); cf. Gordon Gaskill, "Timetable of a Failure," *The Virginia Quarterly Review,* 34, no. 2 (1958): 162–90.

5: RESTORATION AND PRAGMATISM, 1957–68

Despite setbacks in Poland and Hungary, the building of a socialist commonwealth proceeded apace during the decade following the Hungarian revolution, and many Western observers concluded that a secular, open-ended liberalizing trend was producing a consensus which would obviate further displays of Soviet military power. The invasion of Czechoslovakia in August, 1968, imposed a reappraisal of this rather optimistic view, and it affirmed once again the existence of a definite ceiling on pluralistic and voluntaristic tendencies within the system. Nevertheless, if nationalism showed itself to be a far from extinct force in the Eastern Europe of the 1960's, the requirements of economic modernization prompted numerous attempts at coordination and cooperation. The limited but tangible success of these attempts was in the event determined more by regional and pragmatic considerations than by ideological consensus. In the case of Hungary the task of reintegration after the bulk of the nation had unequivocally voiced its preference for a "third road" devolved upon a government subject to almost universal obloquy, but in view of its inauspicious beginnings the Kádár regime proved remarkably adept at adapting communist dogma and reaching an admittedly tenuous *modus vivendi* with the Hungarian people.

Demographic Patterns and the Social Structure

The most striking demographic phenomenon in the postrevolutionary period has been a decline in the natural rate of increase. Whereas between 1931 and 1956 the number of live births per thousand hovered around 20, by 1962 it had reached an all-time low of 12.9, which, taken in conjunction with the death rate, resulted in a natural rate of growth of 2.1 per thousand.[1] Although a decrease in birth rate appears to be concomitant with an advanced stage of economic development, in the case of Hungary the decline was materially affected by the legalization of abortions in 1956. This step was ostensibly taken in the interest of feminine freedom and in order to remove the health hazard of illegal interventions. In practice, by 1959 legal abortions outnumbered live births; between 1959 and 1964 live births dropped by 32 per cent, while legal abortions rose by 900 per cent, giving Hungary the highest abortion rate in Eastern Europe.[2] The immediate effect of this decline was the relative aging of Hungary's population; by 1967 41.1 per cent were forty years of age or over, as opposed to 36.3 per cent in 1949. The economy's future supply of manpower was clearly in jeopardy. In addition, the more intangible question

[1] *Magyar statisztikai zsebkönyv, 1968,* p. 18. Unless otherwise noted, demographic data cited are from this source.

[2] U.S., Bureau of the Census, *Projections of the Population of the Communist Countries of Eastern Europe, by Age and Sex: 1965–1985* (Washington, D.C., 1965), pp. 5–7; see also Radio Free Europe, *The Abortion Problem in Hungary: A Survey* (Background Report), April 7, 1964.

132

of national survival became one of public concern. The maintenance of a cohesive Hungarian nation in the midst of an ethnically alien and often inimical environment had been a recurrent historical problem and a source of collective soul-searching; some even saw in the new policy a conscious effort, dictated by Moscow, to eradicate an intractable and rebellious element from Eastern Europe.[3] Although such apocalyptic rationalizations were rather far-fetched, the regime did take note of the public's dismay at the vital statistics as well as of the latter's possible economic consequences. One official explanation of the decline in live births was the prevalence of working women,[4] and in 1967 the government responded with a program of maternity benefits. Possibly as a result of this policy the birth rate did register a slight rise to 14.6 per thousand in 1967, for a net rate of increase of 0.39 per cent per annum; in 1968 the number of live births rose further, to 15.8 per thousand.

The total population of Hungary on January 1, 1968, stood at 10,236,000; it had incorporated an increase of less than 10 per cent in twenty years. This modest growth was affected not only by natural increase; as a consequence of the revolution some 200,000 Hungarians had left the country, and relatively few have returned to date. On the other hand, some of

[3] Projections based on the 1965 fertility rate (now slightly exceeded in Hungary) showed the following increases in population for the period 1965–85: Albania, 88.6 per cent; Bulgaria, 15.5 per cent; Czechoslovakia, 18.7 per cent; East Germany, 7.6 per cent; *Hungary, 5.8 per cent;* Poland, 26.2 per cent; Rumania, 14.2 per cent; Yugoslavia, 27.0 per cent. See U.S., Bureau of the Census, *Projections of the Population of the Communist Countries of Eastern Europe,* p. 9.

[4] See Zsuzsa Ortutay, "Population Growth and the Family," *Társadalmi Szemle,* 21, no. 10 (1966) : 73–83.

the Magyar minorities in other parts of Eastern Europe have registered a faster rate of growth. In Czechoslovakia, for instance, official statistics show that the proportion of Hungarian nationals rose from 3 per cent in 1950 to 3.9 per cent in 1961, when they numbered 533,934. Rumania had 1,653,700 Hungarians in 1956; Yugoslavia, 504,368 in 1961; and the Ukrainian S.S.R., 149,000 in 1959.[5] Thus, in round figures, some three million Magyars live in proximity to Hungary, for an aggregate total of more than thirteen million in Eastern Europe. Although accurate statistics are lacking, non-Magyar minorities in Hungary account for approximately 4 per cent of the population, including 200,000–220,000 Germans, 100,000–110,000 Slovaks, 80,000–100,000 Yugoslavs, and 20,000–25,000 Rumanians; in 1960 only 23,315 of these persons spoke no Hungarian.[6]

Progressive urbanization has had demographic as well as sociological consequences. At present one-third of the population lives in cities of 40,000 or over, Budapest taking the lion's share with two million inhabitants and accounting for 20 per cent of the total; the 30 per cent increase in the population of these cities since 1949 far surpasses the national figure of 10 per cent, and it represents a rapid rate of urbanization and of rural depopulation, although there are indications that partly as a result of the regime's new agricultural policies the prevailing distribution may

[5] Socialist Federal Republic of Yugoslavia, *Statistical Yearbook, 1967* (Belgrade, 1967), p. 83; Rumania, *Statistical Pocket Book, 1965* (Bucharest, 1965); Czechoslovak Republic, *Statistical Abstract* (Prague, 1965), p. 19; United States Joint Publications Research Service, *The National Economy of the USSR in 1959 (Statistical Yearbook)* (Washington, D.C., 1961), p. 10.

[6] László Kővágó, "The Policy of Our People's Republic Towards Nationalities," *Társadalmi Szemle,* 23, no. 11 (1968): 29–38.

become stabilized.[7] Apart from such major conurbations as Budapest, Miskolc, Pécs, Debrecen, and Szeged, population density is highest in the northern half of the country, with the over-all density in 1968 standing at 110 persons per square kilometer.

The social structure has undergone changes objectively as well as in terms of official ideology. While the cleavage between party élite and masses still prevails, intermediate social groupings have materialized, and relatively value-free empirical methods of social research have received official sanction. Up to 1962 the old monolithic view of the "worker-peasant alliance" was the only permissible orthodoxy; one such breakdown of the social structure put the proportion of workers and employees (including the intelligentsia and pensioners) at 69 per cent (45.7 per cent in 1949), of the peasantry at 27.9 per cent (42.2 per cent in 1949), of craftsmen and tradesmen at 2.3 per cent (8 per cent), and of "others" at 0.8 per cent (1.5 per cent).[8] This analysis, apart from reflecting a decline in the agricultural labor force, concealed the realities of social stratification by failing to differentiate among the groups making up the first category. Since that time sociology as a field of study has acquired legitimate status, notably in the establishment of an institute for sociological research headed by the reformed Stalinist András Hegedüs, and in recent years studies and discussions on stratification, on the family, and on the nature and problems of different social groups have proliferated.[9]

[7] See K. Nagy, "The Impact of Communism in Hungary," p. 13.

[8] László Háy, "Our Society's Class Structure," *Társadalmi Szemle,* 17, no. 12 (1962): 8–17.

[9] See, for instance, András Hegedüs' *A modern polgári szociológia és a társadalmi valóság* (Budapest, 1961), *A szo-*

The basic innovation has been the recognition that the "worker-peasant alliance" did not eradicate socioeconomic differentiation and that differences in income, encouraged by the new economic policies, make the theoretically desirable eradication of social stratification a very long-range goal. This fresh realism comes dangerously close to Western perceptions of class structure and led one party analyst to the somewhat specious clarification that the "difference between us and capitalist societies lies not in that their structure is hierarchical and ours is not, but rather in the qualitative differences that characterize their class-based society."[10]

Whereas the upper class, composed of party élites heading the various institutions, has undergone little qualitative or quantitative change since 1949 and accounts for perhaps 3 per cent of the total population, the emergence of a middle class radically altered the social patterns of the Stalinist era. The phenomenon of this new privileged class, comprising professionals, intellectuals, technocrats, and assorted managers, whose loyalty to the regime is by and large superficial and opportunistic, has been evident in all East European countries. One estimate puts their proportion in Hungary at 15 per cent; since roughly 40 per cent of these were originally manual workers or peasants, some analysts have strived to underline the proletarian roots of the new middle class, but others have observed a progressive pattern of internal recruitment.[11] Educa-

ciológiárol (Budapest, 1966), and "Today's Village and Sociological Research," *Társadalmi Szemle,* 18, no. 4 (1963) : 26–40; cf. Gábor Kiss, "Soziologie in Ungarn," *Osteuropa,* 16, no. 5/6 (1966) : 329–37.

[10] Mrs. Aladár Mód, "Social Stratification in Hungary," *Társadalmi Szemle,* 22, no. 5 (1967) : 15–33.

[11] K. Nagy, "The Impact of Communism in Hungary," p. 14; cf. Sándor Szalai, "Restratification of a Society," *New Hungarian*

tional reforms in 1963 officially removed social origin as a criterion for university entrance; in that year the children of the intelligentsia, employees, and artisans already accounted for 52.4 per cent of the total enrollment in institutes of higher education.[12] Recent studies have noted with some alarm that by 1967 most faculties enrolled half as many children of manual workers and peasants as they had before the reform, and that there were three times as many "good" students from highly educated family backgrounds as from less intellectual backgrounds.[13] Evidently, while a certain discrimination against the old "class enemies" still prevails, new and ideologically more significant obstacles to social mobility have materialized.

Other social problems have drawn the attention of the new sociologists. Their studies of the value system will be considered further on; the role of the family and its partial disintegration, the profound alteration in the way of life of the peasantry, and the agricultural workers' low social and economic status have been some specific sources of concern.[14] The chronic housing shortage, economic dissatisfaction, the growing proportion of working women (39.6 per cent of the labor force in 1967), a prevalence of intergenerational friction and of various forms of collective and individual

Quarterly (Budapest), 7, no. 23 (1966) : 24–33, and Petru Dimitriu, "The Two New Classes," *East Europe,* 10, no. 9 (1961) : 3–6, 30–33.

[12] Dezső Nemes, "The Eighth Party Congress," *Társadalmi Szemle,* 18, no. 2 (1963) : 7–8.

[13] See Béla Köpeczi, "On Some Questions of University Life," *Társadalmi Szemle,* 23, no. 7 (1968) : 12–19, and Ferenc Pataki, "Sociology and the Question of Upbringing," *ibid.,* no. 11 (1968) : 72–82.

[14] Recent statistics show that most of the 170,000 illiterates in Hungary today live in rural areas and include even school-age children; see *Népszabadság,* March 25, 1969.

alienation have all contributed not only to the low birth rate but also to divorce and suicide rates that are among the highest in the world.[15]

Values and Attitudes in Contemporary Hungarian Society

The mass belief system prevailing in Hungary today is a product both of secular trends that are equally in evidence in the West, and of local conditions and historical experiences that are to some extent shared with the other members of the communist system. The revolution and its repression left a profound imprint on the national consciousness; it drove home the unpalatable fact that consensual aspirations for a "third road" were totally incompatible with the realities of the international power balance. An acute feeling of impotence and frustration became manifest after the revolution, leading to widespread alienation and a still-unresolved cleavage between the masses and the ruling élite. With the new thaw that began in 1960 the regime attempted to gain the allegiance of the people by less oppressive and more liberal and constructive measures; this policy of accommodation did achieve some results, but the implantation of a "socialist consciousness" seems to be as remote as ever.

The two phenomena that characterize the belief

[15] See K. Nagy, "The Impact of Communism in Hungary," p. 16. Recent reforms raised to three years the period during which a new mother may take leave of absence from work and receive an allowance, although a few years ago Hegedüs dismissed arguments against working women as representing a bourgeois bias; see András Hegedüs, "The State of the Family and Its Future," *Társadalmi Szemle,* 19, no. 2 (1964) : 43–54.

system are first, a predominance of material over tran-
scendental values, and second, a process of individual-
ization which runs counter to the officially advocated
collectivistic ethic. Both phenomena are to some extent concomitants of modernization; the shift to an
economy geared to mass consumption, the increasingly
urban environment, the decline of the old peasantry
with its traditionalistic behavior patterns, and the transitional atomization that accompanies social restratification are all intrinsic to a society approaching the
contemporary paradigm of development. In the case
of Hungary, materialism has been strengthened by a
rejection of ideologies and by a generally apolitical
predisposition dictated by the system's limited facilities
for popular participation in political decisions. The
long years of material deprivation also contributed to
an insatiable appetite for consumer goods, and acquisition of such status symbols as an automobile has acquired mythical importance. To some extent the government has responded to these demands, thereby
reaping a modicum of support, but its spokesmen have
frequently criticized public opinion for not recognizing
even this admittedly slow rise in the standard of
living.[16]

It is in the realm of ideology that the regime has met
its most striking defeat, and there has been much
debate in party circles over this failure to convert the
masses. Kádár's famous slogan, "who is not against us
is with us," symbolized a liberalization of the dictatorship but elicited opportunistic rather than ideologically
founded allegiance. Explaining that the slogan lets the
individual's labors speak for him, an editor of the

[16] See Mrs. Aladár Mód, "A Few Topical Questions Regarding
the Standard of Living," *Társadalmi Szemle*, 21, no. 3 (1966):
13–27.

party's ideological monthly asked rhetorically, "But if we rule out compulsion and persuasion, how do we educate the people? Partly by the very fact of not *forcing* different views on them."[17] This tolerance, inherent in the regime's new-found pragmatism, clearly relegated mass conversion to the very distant future. In the meantime, commentators have noted that secular trends are leading the mass culture farther away from that goal. One appraisal of the social roots of individualism concludes that the socialist economy has not automatically replaced old-fashioned individualism with a collective social spirit, but has merely provided a foundation for the development of that new spirit.[18]

The failure to imprint a collectivist ethos and the much-discussed question of alienation are receiving increasingly objective consideration, notably by the old populist writer Péter Veres. Writing in the cultural monthly *Kortárs,* Veres conceded that "alienation in the Western sense could be applied to some intellectuals. It could also be applied to a certain extent to all the people who contribute to the building of a socialist society without having a socialist ideology, faith and conviction"; he distinguished alienation, however, from the apolitical apathy of the masses, which "comes from dissatisfaction with the achievements and progress of socialist construction, with the prevalent housing conditions and with homelessness."[19] As a remedy Veres urged greater "familiarization and understanding of public affairs," an open plea for political participation.

[17] Endre Kálmán, "Who Is Not Against Us Is With Us," *Társadalmi Szemle,* 22, no. 2 (1967) : 22–30.

[18] Dr. Dezső Kalocsai, "On the Social Roots of Individualism," *Társadalmi Szemle,* 21, no. 6 (1966) : 106–14.

[19] Péter Veres, "Alienation: A Hungarian View," *East Europe,* 14, no. 3 (1965) : 23–26.

Apart from skepticism, pragmatism, and materialism, behavior patterns also reflect the tenuous legitimacy of the regime and of the socialist economic system. The decline in public morality, for instance, has manifested itself in a marked disrespect for "social" property, and petty and industrial theft represent an endemic problem. The latent opposition to the regime was stressed by Premier Jenő Fock in his last New Year's message: "There are people who do not care for the building of socialism, people living at the expense of society; there are politically indifferent groups and enemies waiting to exploit possible party and government errors; and there are others who consciously act in an unlawful manner, inciting to, organizing and committing political crimes."[20]

The increasing contacts with the West accompanying Kádár's liberalization program have added to the regime's dilemma, for new channels of information have only strengthened the public's capacity for independent comparisons and assessments. The number of visitors from nonsocialist countries rose from 72,039 in 1960 to 498,565 in 1967, while in the same period the number of Hungarians traveling to nonsocialist countries grew from 34,980 to 143,030;[21] in recent years Ford Foundation scholarships have brought numerous Hungarian scholars to the West. Such contacts necessarily highlighted the weaknesses of the official belief system, and while numerous defections occurred, their most important consequence has been to intensify the regime's efforts to overcome popular alienation. Kádár's chief ideologist, Politburo member István Szirmai, attributed the defections to Western propaganda—either direct through Radio Free Europe and the Voice of America, or indirect through the tourists—excoriated

[20] Quoted in *East Europe,* 18, no. 2 (1969) : 45–46.
[21] *MSZ, 1968,* p. 123.

those who left Hungary after receiving a "free" education, and urged that patriotism be identified with the fulfilment of the goal of socialist construction.[22]

The persistence of nationalism as a consensual value has led to official attempts to nurture it in order to gain support and to rechannel it by means of ideologically acceptable associations. In the first case increased expenditures for cultural activities and for the rehabilitation of national monuments, such as the royal palace in Buda, also serve the interests of the booming tourist industry. In the second case, as argued by Politburo member Zoltán Komócsin, the party's position is that the process of building socialism may involve a phase of heightened nationalism, but this must not be interpreted as an anti-Soviet or disintegrative force.[23] Komócsin's observation that strong anti-Soviet elements exist in Hungarian society is supported by a study on the prevalence of nationalism among school children. The author, a teacher, claims that children (in the age group eleven to fourteen) exhibiting nationalistic tendencies are in a minority, but goes on to note that many of them "do not perceive an important, basic difference or contrast between the policies of the Soviet Union and the United States. Some see the Soviet Union primarily as a great power having extensive military capability and political influence."[24] Apparently the children care little for the heroes of the workers' movement, adu-

[22] István Szirmai, "On the Debate Regarding Ideological Directives," *Társadalmi Szemle,* 20, no. 11 (1965) : 1–16; cf. Imre Kovács, "Hungary: The Quest for Respectability," *East Europe,* 14, no. 12 (1965) : 2–8.

[23] *Népszabadság,* March 24, 1966.

[24] Agnes Havas, "Nationalistic Influences on Our Children," *Társadalmi Szemle,* 22, no. 3 (1967) : 97–111. A survey among Hungarian visitors to the West found that more than 80 per cent

lating instead such historical national figures as Rákóczi and Kossuth, and many still voice "irredentist"
sentiments. Apart from a widespread resentment of
Soviet influence, nationalism is also manifested in
a popular (as distinct from official) concern for the
welfare of Magyar minorities in Eastern Europe,
notably in Transylvania, and this will be considered
later on in a different context. A survey conducted in
1968 among young people between the ages of sixteen
and twenty-five offered new evidence of the failure of
indoctrination.[25] Of the sample, 55 per cent were
possessed of a "traditional" value system, 25 per cent
exhibited purely relativistic-individualistic ethics,
while 14 per cent fell into the Marxist-socialist category; thirty-two per cent also voiced a belief in God.

The relative decline of religious faith in what had
been a predominantly Christian society reflects a widespread contemporary phenomenon, but the Kádár
regime has nonetheless tried to reach a compromise
with the churches. The refusal of Cardinal Mindszenty
to leave his refuge in the American Embassy in Budapest and the regime's equally adamant opposition to
his reinstatement have been major obstacles to a nor-
malization of the status of the Roman Catholic church,
although the government continues to provide it with
a modest subsidy. A formal agreement with the Vatican in 1964 did not end the persecution and imprison-
ment of numerous priests and monks; in January, 1969,
a new compromise was reached covering the appoint-

---

were of the opinion that the United States rather than the
Soviet Union was the "most influential" country in the world;
see "What Do East Europeans Think?" *East Europe,* 15, no. 3
(1966) : 26–28.

[25] Gábor Czakó, "Twenty-year-old Morality," *Kortárs,* 12, no.
11 (1968) : 1729–42.

ment of ten bishops and apostolic administrators, and a few seminaries and Catholic secondary schools still survive, but the freedom of the churches remains closely circumscribed. A recent conference in Budapest on the sociology of religion concluded that while religion was a false transnational integrative concept, religious faith would remain for some time a factor to contend with and that, consequently, socialism had to be built with the cooperation of believers.[26] Finally, it must be noted that anti-Semitism (and a traditional contempt for Gypsies) is as much in evidence in Hungary as it is in the other socialist societies. Kádár's de-Stalinization removed most of the Jews from high party positions, and in any event they account for only about 2 per cent of the population, but, as in the past, their predominance in the professions and other privileged functions makes them the subject of popular prejudice.[27]

In view of the catalytic role that it had played prior to the revolution, the literary establishment predictably suffered an eclipse in the early restoration period. Many of the writers fled; most of the others, tainted by their open advocacy of Nagy's brand of revisionism, were forced to withdraw into mute isolation.[28] Even György Lukács, whose support for Nagy had been noticeably timid, was marked as a *persona non grata* and could not publish in Hungary until 1964; in an interview that year for a Prague literary weekly, he declared that "first, we must show the world

[26] József Lukács, "The International Conference in Budapest on the Sociology of Religion," *Társadalmi Szemle,* 23, no. 6 (1968) : 82–89.

[27] Cf. François Fejtő, *Les Juifs et l'antisémitisme dans les pays communistes* (Paris, 1960).

[28] See Váli, *Rift and Revolt in Hungary,* pp. 453–57.

what Marxism is in contrast to stalinism."[29] Three years later Lukács was readmitted to the party, but the regime has consistently kept the old philosopher at arm's length. Even after Kádár relaxed the strictures against them, many of the writers manifested their disillusionment with the system by limiting their output to ostensibly apolitical works dealing increasingly with the question of individual alienation.

The party's new literary policy, promulgated in the early sixties, gave writers the freedom to criticize Stalinism (and, of course, "bourgeois counterrevolution") as long as they did not identify it with existing policies, and subsequently censorship became less centralized and pervasive.[30] The official sanction for stylistic diversity produced some confusion, for in the absence of strict ideological guidelines the self-discipline of the writers was bound to have its lapses. As early as 1963 Szirmai complained that "bourgeois" writers had abused the new policy;[31] two years later Komócsin castigated the press for its insufficient ideological content, all the while defending the function of "justified criticism."[32] In a study on the social function of art and literature, the party's "Cultural Theoretical Working Group" noted the public's tendency to look for evidence of social and ideological criticism, and defended socialist realism in terms of its commitment

[29] "George Lukács on Stalinism and Art," *East Europe,* 13, no. 5 (1964) : 22–26; cf. François Fejtő, "Georges Lukács," *Esprit,* February, 1961.

[30] William Juhász, "Writers and Politics," *East Europe,* 12, no. 7 (1963) : 6–14; cf. László M. Tikos, "Hungary: Literary Renascence," *Problems of Communism,* 13, no. 3 (1964) : 24–34.

[31] *Népszabadság,* March 30, 1963.

[32] Zoltán Komócsin, "Ideological Directives and the Press," *Társadalmi Szemle,* 20, no. 7 (1965) : 1–9.

145

and partisanship; at the same time, irrationalist, decadent, and absurd manifestations were censured for being tailored to snobbish, Western-oriented bourgeois tastes.[33] The group also noted that an earlier emphasis on the publication of Hungarian classics (presumed to be safely remote from ideological controversy) had backfired by rooting popular tastes in the nineteenth century, and it urged corrective action by the mass media. Evidently the conflicting values of artistic license and of self-imposed censorship have yet to be reconciled, although the ever-present threat of official disgrace and a consequent loss of livelihood remains a powerful deterrent. Older populists, such as Veres and Illyés, continue to produce, and even "bourgeois" authors survive by writing patently nonpolitical works; as Kádár recently told the executive council of the Hungarian Writers' Association, writers may enjoy creative freedom, but in any conflict between bourgeois and working-class interests they must defend the latter.[34] In recent years there has emerged a new generation of writers—exemplified by Sándor Csoóri and Erzsébet Galgóczi—who are establishing a neo-populist tradition with their revealing social and psychological studies of the peasantry.[35]

One of many cultural manifestations, publishing finds a ready public in Hungary; in 1967 a total of 4,714 works (for an aggregate of 47.8 million copies) found their way into print.[36] At the same time, cultural Russification has been eased. Out of a total of 644 literary

[33] "The Function of Literature and Art in Our Society," *Társadalmi Szemle*, 21, no. 7/8 (1966) : 29–58.

[34] *Népszabadság*, June 9, 1968.

[35] See Ferenc Erdei, "On Today's Literary Sociography," *Kortárs*, 8, no. 5 (1964) : 831–34.

[36] *MSZ, 1968*, pp. 187–97.

works published in 1967, only 50 had been translated from Russian. Attendance at classical concerts and theatrical productions in 1967 approached the seven million mark, while in that same year the number of television subscribers reached 1,168,800 and the circulation of daily newspapers stood at more than two million. Thus, at least in quantitative terms, the availability of cultural events and of mass media places Hungary among the most advanced societies in the world. But the removal of all qualitative restraints remains unlikely as long as the Communist Party claims a monopoly of ideological orthodoxy.

Ideological Reappraisals and the Political System

For some time after Soviet troops had pacified the country, there prevailed among the higher echelons of the reformed Hungarian Socialist Workers' Party a state of ideological vacillation and ambivalence. Kádár's personal experience with the most inhuman aspects of Stalinism, and the ongoing de-Stalinization campaign in the Soviet Union, seemed to preclude a return to old-style dogmatism; as for Titoist revisionism, the revolution had demonstrated that, at least in the Hungarian context, it led to a rejection of Marxism-Leninism, and consequently a meaningful accommodation with the Nagy faction appeared equally impracticable. This dilemma was further complicated by the numerical weakness of the new leadership, which prevented Kádár from immediately repudiating those members of the old guard who had survived the revolution. A Stalinist counterattack was launched in March, 1957, by Révai, who demanded that earlier concessions to the workers' councils be repudiated, ob-

147

served that at their worst Rákosi and Gerő had never been guilty of treason—for which sin Nagy had to be condemned without reservations—and warned that any nationalism which weakened loyalty to the Soviet Union was considered purely reactionary.[37]

Although Kádár had no choice but to include Stalinists such as Révai and Antal Apró and even some Nagy sympathizers in his new apparat, he persisted in denouncing the Rákosists and refused to rehabilitate Gerő and the other exiles; in this action his hand was strengthened by Khrushchev's successful stand against the "anti-party group" in June, 1967, and, when it became clear that he was Khrushchev's man in Hungary, the influence of the dogmatists gradually waned. Any rapprochement with Tito was also out of the question. The Moscow twelve-party declaration of November, 1957, reaffirmed the campaign against revisionism, and the "trial" and execution of Nagy, Maléter, et al. the following year cast a final verdict on the revolution.[38] In 1959 the party's Seventh Congress pointedly referred to the dangers of revisionism.[39] It was another four years before a meeting between Kádár and Tito provided the occasion for a cautious reconciliation.

Internally, the first few years of the Kádár regime represented a period of consolidation marked by punitive measures against revolutionaries young and old, by a drastic and effective collectivization campaign, and by a profound cleavage between the party and the masses. The subsequent shift to a more liberal, "cen-

[37] *Népszabadság,* March 7, 1957.
[38] *Pravda,* November 22, 1957; *Népszabadság,* June 17, 1958.
[39] See William E. Griffith, "The Decline and Fall of Revisionism in Eastern Europe," in *Revisionism,* ed. Leopold Labedz (New York, 1962), pp. 223–38.

trist" line coincided with the Twenty-second Congress of the CPSU in 1961, which again singled out sectarianism (i.e., Stalinism) as the main enemy. There ensued in Hungary a debate between secularizers and ideologists, and the reforms of the past few years indicate that the pragmatism of the former, exemplified by Kádár himself, has prevailed. In keeping with its nonideological nature, the regime's centrist orientation has been manifested in a number of specific reforms and changes in personnel rather than in explicitly doctrinal terms. Ideological reappraisals require scapegoats, and in 1962 three hard-liners, Marosán, Károly Kiss, and Imre Dögei (the last-named having been responsible for collectivization), were removed from the leadership; significantly, the new stress on "socialist legality" prevented their liquidation, and today even old Stalinists, such as the Farkases (Sr. and Jr.), prosper in retirement.[40] At the other end of the political spectrum, most political prisoners have been amnestied, Bibó being released in 1963 and allowed to eke out a living as a librarian.

In essence, Kádár's centrism is a pragmatic and eclectic disposition to strengthen the legitimacy of his regime by concentrating on economic modernization and by depoliticizing certain administrative functions. There have been few structural changes—collective farms still prevail in the agricultural sector—although the "New Economic Mechanism" that was put into effect in 1968 represents a significant innovation. The more functional aspects of the system, on the other hand, have undergone a major transformation. The

[40] On the debate regarding jurisprudence and "socialist legality," see G. R. Urban, "Hungary," in *Polycentrism*, ed. Walter Laqueur and Leopold Labedz (New York, 1962), pp. 75–76.

149

class struggle has been reinterpreted to mean simply a drive for efficiency, and the old qualifications of explicit ideological orthodoxy and working-class origins have been to some extent supplanted by a new stress on expertise.[41] As Kádár put it to a workers' meeting in 1962: "Many sorts of people with many different pasts and views live together with us in our people's system. They live and work honourably, each in his own field. . . . They do not harm us—we only fight those who attack the people's power."[42] Concurrently, discrimination against kulaks and within the educational system has been relaxed, if not eliminated; following the disbandment of the AVH, the old police terror also faded away, although a branch of the Ministry of Interior carries on its less overt functions.

Since the application of objective criteria of proficiency potentially weakened the party's monopoly on positions of responsibility, it was to be expected that middle-level apparatchiks would feel threatened; in order to pacify the latter there have been numerous appeals directed at the new middle-class experts to exhibit correct ideological consciousness, but the general effect of the reforms has been to secularize many administrative and professional activities.[43] This prag-

[41] The Rákosi regime had endowed the state administration with numerous high officials whose incompetence and low level of education (many had not even completed secondary school) had been outweighed by political considerations, as shown by some remarkable statistics in *Figyelő*, May 27, 1958, cited in Brzezinski, *The Soviet Bloc*, p. 143. Cf. A. J. von Lazar, "Class Struggle and Socialist Construction: The Hungarian Paradox," *Slavic Review*, 25, no. 2 (1966) : 303–13.

[42] *Népszabadság*, March 4, 1962, cited in Urban, "Hungary," p. 78.

[43] See *Népszabadság*, September 2, 1964. In 1966 a Scientific Qualification Committee was set up to ensure the ideological relevance of research; see *East Europe*, 15, no. 5 (1966) : 49.

matic ethos has contributed to the progressive isolation of the largely incompetent old-guard functionaries and to an infusion of younger reformers, such as Rezső Nyers, into the leadership. Nevertheless, pragmatism has to be reconciled with the leading role of the party, and this occasions frequent reappraisals highlighting the ever-present cleavage between the élite and the other social groupings. From a prerevolution high of 900,000, total party membership fell to 96,000 in December, 1956 (a more realistic approximation of its loyal clientele); since that time it has risen to its present strength of around 600,000 card-carrying members, who represent close to 6 per cent of the population. It has been estimated that manual workers account for 35 per cent, collective members for 16 per cent, and technocrats and intellectuals for 15 per cent of the membership.[44] Although the relatively low representation of the "worker-peasant alliance" has elicited rather self-conscious reassertions of the importance of working-class support,[45] in recent practice the emphasis has been on the recruitment of middle-class members. Indications are, however, that the party is becoming an increasingly remote and autonomous institution; at the Eighth Congress in November, 1962, fully 69 per cent of the delegates were members of the apparat, while in the 101-member Central Committee elected in 1966, 35 seats were allocated to the party apparatus, 10 to mass organizations, 32 to the state apparatus, and 24 to other groups and members at large.[46] Notwithstanding the relative isolation of

[44] György Máté, "Thoughts on the Evolution of Our Party's Composition," *Társadalmi Szemle,* 19, no. 2 (1964) : 33–42.

[45] See Ferenc Kovács, "Debate on the Concept of the Working Class," *Társadalmi Szemle,* 23, no. 1 (1968) : 70–77.

[46] François Fejtő, "Hungarian Communism," p. 214; Magyar Távirati Iroda (MTI) release, December 7, 1966.

the party, the link with the working class is still evident in the composition of the Politburo. Of the eleven members and four alternate members, all but two come from a working-class or peasant background, and few have had the benefit of formal higher education; most of them represent the old "indigenous" wing of the party.[47]

In the debate on the question of nonparty experts and technocrats, the self-styled sociologist András Hegedüs has played the devil's advocate by arguing that in the present stage of socialist evolution a secular bureaucracy must be accepted as inevitable, and that the necessary "social supervision" will have to be provided by a new "overseer" type of party; more orthodox leaders have stressed that the party must remain the ruling and guiding organ and must therefore fight for the allegiance of the working classes and other social groupings.[48] This uneasiness regarding the function of the party is clearly intensified by the independent evolution of the mass belief system. While the party refrains from openly condemning patriotism, and indeed tries to identify its objectives with that sentiment, Kádár has frequently censured those elements which expect De Gaulle's brand of European nationalism to break up the socialist bloc; he has also attacked materialists and secularizers who seek to undermine the system by positing a spurious convergence of practical Marxism and bourgeois values.[49]

[47] Sándor Kiss, "The Kádár Imprint on the Hungarian Party," *East Europe*, 18, no. 3 (1969) : 5–8.

[48] István Friss, "Class Struggle, State, Party, and Social Development," *Kortárs*, 12, no. 10 (1968) : 1599–1609; cf. Ferenc Erdei, "Expertness and Democracy," *Társadalmi Szemle*, 22, no. 5 (1967) : 3–14, and William F. Robinson, "Hungary's Turn to Revisionism," *East Europe*, 16, no. 9 (1967) : 14–18.

[49] In an interview with UPI correspondent Henry Shapiro on

Since the party is still fighting, as Rezső Nyers declared at the Ninth Congress in 1966, for the political unity of the working class[50] the system's organs for mobilizing support are of key importance. The concurrent pressures for popular participation in policy-making mean, however, that the old mass organizations, acting as uni-directional and unresponsive channels of indoctrination, no longer suffice. A case in point is the KISZ (Communist Youth League, with a membership of around 750,000), which a 1964 survey found to be ineffective in its function of influencing young people.[51] New members are no longer required to be ideologically perfect, and in 1968 the organization held a "parliament" of young collective workers who proceeded to air various economic grievances.[52] The regime's constant dilemma is that such dissent, if encouraged, may eventually challenge the party. The Patriotic People's Front (with 3,500 local committees and 130,000 members) has had the long-standing function of strengthening the democratic image of the system, and was called upon recently to mobilize support for the economic reforms, but it too has been sub-

---

July 27, 1966, Kádár declared: "Since the building of socialism proceeds within national boundaries, it necessarily follows that its success will foster national self-respect and patriotic pride. This, however, is not identical with nationalism. . . . The imperialists . . . are now trying to separate certain socialist countries from each other, from the Soviet Union, by stimulating nationalism. These machinations are bound to fail, for the community of interests and shared ideology of our countries are stronger than any nationalistic provocation, and will prevail over the latter" (János Kádár, *Hazafiság és internacionalizmus* [Budapest, 1968], p. 220) . See also Kádár's speech to the National Assembly, *Népszabadság*, February 12, 1965.

[50] Rezső Nyers, "The Congress of Progress, Peace, and Socialism," *Társadalmi Szemle*, 21, no. 12 (1966) : 3–12.

[51] *Magyar Nemzet*, May 17, 1964.

[52] *Népszabadság*, January 19, 1968.

ject to pluralistic pressures. At its Fourth Congress in 1968 a suggestion was voiced that the front should become more active politically by actually proposing new legislation to Parliament.[53] Even public-opinion research seems to be acquiring a grudging acceptance in party circles;[54] in October, 1967, party activists reportedly carried out an opinion poll among the membership. The possibility that such experiments might lead to structural changes has been emphatically denied, notably by Dezső Nemes, the last remaining Muscovite in the Politburo: "Only a few reactionary elements desire a multiparty system, those who hope that in this way they may operate more effectively in breaking up the political unity and creative forces of the nation."[55] Nemes argued that the party and other existing organizations provided ample representation.

As early as 1963, however, the Kádár regime was considering tentative proposals for changes in the political process to increase popular participation. Addressing the party's Political Academy, Gyula Kállai, a Politburo member and deputy premier, noted the possibility of extending the planning and advisory functions of organizations such as the National Council of Trade-Unions and the Cooperatives Council and even of having candidates compete for election.[56] Four years later Kádár manifested a new awareness of pluralistic tendencies by telling the Central Committee that, in addition to the individual and the entire society, the

[53] See *East Europe,* 17, no. 6 (1968) : 46–47.

[54] See Edit S. Molnár, "Public-Opinion Research and Social Life," *Társadalmi Szemle,* 21, no. 4 (1966) : 84–91.

[55] Dezső Nemes, "The Development of Socialist Democracy in Hungary," *Társadalmi Szemle,* 19, no. 11 (1964) : 19–44.

[56] *Népszabadság,* April 21, 1963.

collective interests of certain socioeconomic
ought also to be taken into consideration.[57]

In the meantime, in November, 1966, the Ninth
Party Congress had approved a modified electoral system for both parliamentary and local council elections,
creating individual polling districts and allowing for
the nomination of several candidates; the Patriotic
People's Front was charged with sponsoring the nomination meetings and supervising the balloting.[58] In the
March, 1967, elections only nine parliamentary con-
stituencies had two aspirants, and all nine "opposition"
candidates were defeated. The omnipotence of the
party stood unaltered, both the prime minister (Jenő
Fock) and the president of the National Assembly
(Kállai) being also full members of the Politburo.[59]
Deputy Premier Antal Apró had hinted at the 1966
congress that Parliament might take a more active part
in the investigation of problems and the preparation
of legislation,[60] and indeed the question period and
the committee system have been revitalized within
certain qualitative limits, but any genuine decentrali-

[57] János Kádár, "Statement at the November 24 Meeting of the
Central Committee," *Társadalmi Szemle*, 22, no. 12 (1967) : 25.

[58] See Ottó Bihari, "Hungary's New Electoral Law," *New
Hungarian Quarterly*, 8, no. 26 (1967) : 94–104.

[59] In the Politburo elected by the Ninth Party Congress in
November, 1966, the following were full members: János Kádár
(first secretary), Béla Biszku (secretary), Zoltán Komócsin
(secretary), Rezső Nyers (secretary), Antal Apró (also deputy
premier), Lajos Fehér (also deputy premier), Jenő Fock (also
premier), Sándor Gáspár (also secretary-general of the National
Council of Trade-Unions), Gyula Kállai, Dezső Nemes, and
István Szirmai. Alternate members were Miklós Ajtai (also
deputy premier), Lajos Czinege (also minister of defense), Pál
Ilku (also minister of culture), and Károly Németh.

[60] *Népszabadság*, November 12, 1966.

zation and pluralism within the political system remains highly unlikely. The locus of effective decision-making lies within the party leadership, and for the moment the dominant position of Kádár's centrist wing appears secure. There are indications, however, that public opinion is becoming more assertive, with the trade-unions representing a potential source for the articulation of dissent. The effective challenge by transport workers and mailmen of two decrees of the Ministry of Transport and Telecommunications in July, 1968, suggests that Kádár's tentative recognition of the rights of socioeconomic groups (added to the decentralizing impetus of the New Economic Mechanism) may yet backfire.[61]

From Collectivization to the New Economic Mechanism

Peasant dissatisfaction with the collective system of farming led to an exodus from the kolkhoz during the revolution, and for two years thereafter farmers enjoyed relative freedom from official pressures and compulsory deliveries. Approximately 70 per cent of the arable land was in the private sector, and agricultural production rose at a sustained, if unspectacular, pace. Despite the opposition of most economists and some party elements, the decision was taken early in 1959 (following Kádár's visit to the Twenty-first Congress of the CPSU) to bring Hungary's agriculture system back into line with that prevailing in the rest of the Communist bloc (with the exception of Poland), and

[61] *Népszava*, July 7, 1968.

Kádár

a massive re-collectivization campaign was initiated. Forceful measures overcame the reluctance of the peasantry, and by 1967 the socialist sector accounted for 97.1 per cent, and collective farms for 80.4 per cent, of all arable land.[62]

The economic and social consequences of the new collectivization were little short of disastrous. The second Five-Year Plan had scheduled an increase of 22 per cent in agricultural production; despite heavy investments in agricultural machinery and the adoption of the "Nádudvar" system of incentives in kind,[63] production had risen only 10 per cent by the end of the plan period in 1965. In contrast, household plots (accounting for 9.8 per cent of arable land) produced 46 per cent of all meat, 79 per cent of the poultry, 90 per cent of the eggs, 60 per cent of the milk, and bore 80 per cent of the fruit trees (except apple) in Hungary. As a result, even the Central Committee warned against underestimating the contribution of household plots.[64] Bad weather conditions in 1963 and 1964 and the calculated indolence of the peasantry contributed to small harvests and necessitated the purchase of nine million bushels of grain from Canada over a three-year period. The decline in grain production to well below prewar levels was due in part to a transfer of land to other uses, notably meat production, which in the event enjoyed a healthier rate of growth. Meanwhile, the inimical atmosphere of the collectives and the lure of better-paying jobs in industry occasioned a drop in

2nd 5 year plan

[62] *MSZ, 1968,* p. 72.
[63] See Fred E. Dohrs, "Incentives in Communist Agriculture: The Hungarian Models," *Slavic Review,* 27, no. 1 (1968) : 23–38.
[64] Central Committee resolution, *Népszabadság,* February 23, 1964.

the number of agricultural workers from 1,925,100 in 1960 to 1,493,900 in 1967; at the same time the workers' average age rose to over fifty.[65]

In the industrial sector the second Five-Year Plan came closer to fulfillment, with production growing by 47 per cent in that period; higher norms, tighter labor discipline, and a much slower rise in real wages resulted in widespread discontent within the labor force. The plan did moderate the Stalinist emphasis on heavy industry by increasing investments in the more labor-intensive areas (notably in telecommunications), and in spite of occasional obstructionism by conservative apparatchiks the new policy favoring nonparty experts improved managerial efficiency. A drive to increase productivity was launched concurrently with the plan, with party leaders calling for more competition and incentives to encourage modernization of the physical plant;[66] following the Yugoslav model, a 5 per cent interest charge was applied on the value of the fixed and working capital of industrial enterprises, again in the interests of economy and efficiency. Nevertheless, an unfavorable balance of trade prevailed between 1960 and 1965, and the national income, with an increase of 25 per cent, fell far short of the projected rise of 36 per cent.

By the last year of the plan the declining rate of growth had caused sufficient alarm among the ruling circles to stimulate a major reappraisal of economic planning. In the summer of 1957 the Kádár regime had set up eleven committees of economists under István Varga to advise upon a reconstruction and

[65] Sándor Kiss, "Hungarian Agriculture Under the NEM," *East Europe*, 17, no. 8 (1968) : 11.

[66] See, for instance, Nyers' statement in *Népszabadság*, March 12, 1964.

modernization program (the revolution having cost Hungary one-fifth of her gross national product). Their report included proposals for decentralization and a wider use of the profit incentive—much along the lines of the subsequent Liberman approach—but at the time such reforms appeared far too radical.[67] Eight years later the Politburo's economic expert, Rezső Nyers, offered a virtually identical solution to Hungary's economic problems.[68] The new proposals included an attenuation of the "price bureaucracy" by a means of a three-tier pricing system providing fixed prices for raw materials, food, and certain products, maximum rates for other specified products, and a free price system for the rest; a closer correspondence of wages and profits, an investment policy according to which only major projects would be financed directly out of the state budget, and more independence for the collectives in their investments were also among the proposed reforms.[69] The Yugoslav practice of worker-administration in the enterprises was rejected in favor of a more intangible participation by the workers in policy-making.[70]

These new concepts were not immediately implemented, but the third Five-Year Plan embodied fewer guidelines and more realistic projections, and it emphasized productivity as well as a decentralization of responsibility. In May, 1966, the Central Committee

[67] István Varga, "The Report of the Committee of Economic Experts," *Közgazdasági Szemle,* 4, no. 10 (1957) : 997–1008 and no. 12 (1957) : 1231–47; cf. J. Kornai, *A gazdasági vezetés túlzott központosítása* (Budapest, 1957).

[68] Rezső Nyers, "Problems of Our Economic Planning System," *Társadalmi Szemle,* 20, no. 7 (1965) : 10–29.

[69] *Népszabadság,* November 21, 1965.

[70] Dr. József Szabó, "On Economic Democracy," *Társadalmi Szemle,* 21, no. 12 (1966) : 13–27.

NEM

approved a long-range program for economic reform known as the New Economic Mechanism, which was to come into effect in 1968.[71] Although there are signs of a more long-run economic revival, the first year of the NEM showed an only marginal improvement in industrial productivity.[72] Decentralization has also brought about certain possibly transitional difficulties. Jurisdictional disputes—between party cadres and managers, and between the latter and the unions—have multiplied. One party expert noted judiciously that "it will not always be easy to decide in a free pricing system whether a rise in prices represents an adjustment to the market which will lead to higher production and better satisfaction of the demand, or whether it represents a form of speculation."[73] Nor is it likely that the regime will in the short run sacrifice patently unproductive enterprises. In the drive for profits and productivity the workers may be short-changed; although according to the new labor code trade-unions have increased powers to negotiate with management and may even veto the latter's decisions,[74] the importance of premiums in the workers' incomes and the shortage of funds available for

[71] Népszabadság, May 29, 1966.

[72] Ibid., February 2, 1969; cf. Barnabás A. Rácz, "Assessing Hungary's Economic Reforms," East Europe, 17, no. 12 (1968): 2–9.

[73] Dr. György Kálmán, "The Function of Legal Instruments in the New System of Economic Planning," Társadalmi Szemle, 23, no. 1 (1968): 70–77.

[74] See William Sólyom-Fekete, "Hungary's New Labor Code," East Europe, 17, no. 2 (1968): 17–20, and Sándor Gáspár, "Trade-Union Problems in Hungary," World Marxist Review (Prague), 11, no. 6 (1968): 8–11. In a speech before the Central Committee on November 24, 1967, Kádár observed with some anticipation that the success of the reform "depends upon

plant modernization give managers the power and the incentive to exploit the labor force. The dependent status of the National Council of Trade-Unions ensures that individual and group interests will take second place to the over-all objectives of the national economy.[75] The greater productivity is aimed at achieving a more advantageous balance of trade rather than at significantly raising the standard of living; although the latter is among the highest in the Communist bloc, shortages in housing and in certain consumer products and foodstuffs for the home market remain unresolved, despite the recent creation of an equally dependent "Consumers' Council."

One positive result of the NEM has been an improvement in the relative position of the agricultural sector. The reforms (projected or already in force) include a guaranteed monthly income for peasants, a reduction in the income gap between industrial and agricultural workers, a graduated tax system that would assist less productive collectives, the manufacture of small-farm machinery to increase the already high productivity of household plots, and a transfer of the ownership of land to the collectives in order to enhance their independence; the interests of the collectives are theoretically furthered by the National Council of Agricultural Cooperatives, an organization

two-three hundred thousand managers. I am glad that our relations with them are based on mutual trust, which is indispensable at this point" (Kádár, "Statement at the November 24 Meeting of the Central Committee," p. 23). The regime took the precaution of strengthening that trust by means of a differentiated system of profit-sharing which allows managers an annual premium of up to 80 per cent of the normal salaries, while the figure for professionals and technicians is 50 per cent, that for workers 15 per cent.

[75] See Rácz, "Assessing Hungary's Economic Reforms," pp. 6–7.

established in 1967.[76] Although the centralized credit system and the party's network of rural operatives have a disincentive effect, there are indications that the exodus from the farms has stopped and that the peasantry is better off than it has been since 1958. Indeed, within the last two years several agricultural collectives have taken the unprecedented initiative of entering the field of light manufacturing, as if to demonstrate that the entrepreneurial spirit is far from dead in Hungary.

In sum, the NEM appears to be lifting Hungary out of its economic stagnation.[77] Industrial productivity is still well below that of the more developed European countries; the dearth of managerial expertise, the small home market, and, more significantly, the necessarily

[76] See Kiss, "Hungarian Agriculture Under the NEM," pp. 12–18; cf. Dr. Imre Tar, "Toward the Development of Land Ownership," *Társadalmi Szemle,* 22, no. 1 (1967) : 25–31.

[77] This stagnation is also borne out by comparative data. Between 1963 and 1966 Hungary's per capita product (at constant prices) grew by 14 per cent; the corresponding rate for Bulgaria was 28 per cent, for Czechoslovakia 12 per cent, for East Germany 18 per cent, for Poland 20 per cent, for Rumania 32 per cent, and for Yugoslavia 22 per cent. United Nations, *Statistical Yearbook, 1967* (New York, 1968). In the same period, Hungary's per capita consumption had the fastest, her industrial productivity the lowest, rate of growth in the Communist bloc. Although such comparisons are subject to statistical inaccuracies, it is also worth noting that, whereas in 1938 the consumption per capita in Hungary stood at 87 per cent of that in Germany, the ratio (with respect to West Germany) has been declining steadily since 1950, to 48 per cent in 1964. In that year, Hungary's gross national product per capita was estimated at U.S. $880, compared to $600 for Bulgaria, $1,280 for Czechoslovakia, $1,220 for East Germany, $770 for Poland, and $590 for Rumania. See U.S., Congress, Joint Economic Committee, *New Directions in the Soviet Economy,* 89th Cong., 2d sess., 1966, pt. 4: Maurice Ernst, "Postwar Economic Growth in Eastern Europe (A Comparison with Western Europe)," pp. 873–916; cf. Václav Holešovský, "Personal Consumption in Czechoslovakia, Hungary, and Poland, 1950–1960: A Comparison," *Slavic Review,* 24, no. 4 (1965) : 622–35.

slow increase in investments, represent bottlenecks to which there is no rapid remedy in sight.[78] Lack of adequate local sources of energy has long hampered industrial development, but the growing utilization of natural gas may reduce costs; cheaper access to Iranian oil may also benefit the burgeoning petrochemicals industry. At present, industry (including construction) provides approximately 66 per cent, and agriculture 22 per cent, of the gross national product; the socialist sector accounts for 97.3 per cent of the national income.[79] Industry employs 32.3 per cent of the labor force, construction 6.5 per cent, agriculture 30.9 per cent, transportation 6.5 per cent, commerce 7.0 per cent, and other sectors and occupations 16.8 per cent; as a result of discriminatory policies, the number of self-employed artisans had by 1967 dwindled to 71,996 from a high of 123,187 ten years earlier. The proportional contribution to the total industrial production (state enterprises) in mining is 6 per cent, in the electrical power-generating industry 5 per cent, in metallurgy 12 per cent, in heavy machinery 25 per cent, in construction material 3 per cent, in chemicals 11 per cent, in light manufacturing 17 per cent, and in the food processing industry 21 per cent.[80]

Progress and Limitations of Economic Integration

As we noted in Chapter 3, the integrative institutions of the Stalinist period were empty shells that only

[78] See Premier Fock's report in *Népszabadság,* October 17, 1968.

[79] *MSZ, 1968,* p. 38. At the official (and unrealistic) rate of exchange, Hungary's gross national income in 1968 stood at approximately $18 billion.

[80] *Ibid.,* pp. 135, 60.

symbolized the real links between the Soviet Union and its client states in Eastern Europe. The establishment in January, 1949, of the Council for Mutual Economic Assistance (CEMA, otherwise known as Comecon) had no immediate effect on the internal economic development of Hungary, and the concurrent reorientation of her trade was implemented through bilateral treaties that owed little to the existence of CEMA. While Stalin ruled, his policies favoring autarchic development over genuine multilateralism prevailed throughout the area;[81] within the resulting loosely coordinated trade mechanism, the Soviet Union dictated the terms of trade, and local advantages in the factors of production were seldom taken into consideration. The first, tentative steps toward specialization came out of the 1954 CEMA meetings, although the actual negotiations were still carried out bilaterally. In that year Hungary signed agreements with Czechoslovakia and with Rumania for coordination in the production of aluminum and chemicals. Other bilateral negotiations regarding intraproduct specialization led to agreements with Czechoslovakia and Poland on rolled steel and with Rumania on ball bearings in 1954, and with East Germany and Czechoslovakia on manufactured consumer goods in the following year.

In the immediate post-Stalin period the concept of a "socialist commonwealth" began to make some headway.[82] At CEMA's seventh session, in May, 1956, the institution was expanded through the creation of thirteen standing commissions (one of which, Nonferrous Metallurgy, was headquartered in Budapest), which

[81] See I. Nagy, *On Communism*, p. 189.
[82] For an analytical history of CEMA, see Michael Kaser, *Comecon* (London, 1965).

were charged with recommending areas of specialization. The Rome Treaty of 1957 provided a further stimulus for genuine integration, while, concurrently, the new Khrushchevian orthodoxy recognized that the earlier "universalization" of each economy had been costly and unjustified.[83] The Soviet Union had proposed a joint economic plan for the entire area early in 1956, and at the CEMA meeting specialization in industrial production came under discussion. At the time, Hungary's position stood halfway between that of Czechoslovakia and East Germany, whose well-developed industrial infrastructure made such a division of labor seem attractive, and that of Poland and Rumania, who expressed strong reservations; the negative factor of her limited stage of industrialization and modernization and the positive factor of her heavy reliance on trade (only East Germany and Czechoslovakia had a higher per capita index of foreign trade) led to Hungary's qualified endorsement of the meeting's recommendations.

The upheavals of 1956 created a hiatus in the drive for economic integration, but at a meeting two years later the party leaders of the CEMA states once again agreed on general recommendations for the coordination of production and trade policies. (Meanwhile, in 1957 all CEMA members except Albania, Mongolia, and Rumania had granted credits totaling $295.7 million to assist in Hungary's economic recovery.) As a result of these recommendations, by the end of 1958 bilateral agreements linked Hungary with most of the other members; coordinative efforts in more specific

[83] Grzybowski, *Socialist Commonwealth of Nations*, pp. 91–92; cf. József Bognár and Imre Vajda, "Problems of International Labor Division among the Socialist Countries," *Közgazdasági Szemle*, 5, no. 1 (1958) : 34–55.

areas included an abortive agreement with Czechoslovakia to build hydroelectric installations on the Danube and a plan for Hungarian investment in Bulgarian
iron ore. In addition, Hungary participated in the
establishment of intergovernmental commissions on
economic, scientific, and technical collaboration with
Bulgaria, Poland, and Rumania in 1958, with Czechoslovakia in 1961, with East Germany in 1962, and with
the Soviet Union in 1964. All these measures, however, fell far short of genuine multilateral coordination
and cooperation.[84]

The major impetus toward economic integration
came with the declaration on "Basic Principles of the
International Socialist Division of Labor" which issued
out of the CEMA conference in Moscow in June,
1962.[85] Plan coordination, the elimination of differences in economic development, and interstate specialization were set down as desirable goals, ostensibly so
that all the member states could make the ultimate
transition to communism simultaneously. At the same
time there came into being an executive committee
(composed of a deputy premier from each member,
Antal Apró in the case of Hungary), which was to meet
every three months and act as the supreme decision-
making organ of CEMA, as well as an expanded permanent secretariat in Moscow.

Hardly had CEMA come to approximate a truly
supranational institution, however, than the resurgent
economic nationalism exemplified by Rumania set new
limits to the movement toward integration. Partly in
consequence of Rumania's intransigence, a new doc-

[84] For developments up to 1960, see László Zsoldos, *Economic
Integration of Hungary into the Soviet Bloc* (Columbus, Ohio,
1963).

[85] McNeal, *International Relations Among Communists,* pp.
125–27.

trine materialized which hinged on the independent variable of the "interested party," and since 1964 the consensus has been that multilateral problems would be resolved within the framework of CEMA only when all parties were indeed interested and willing. Grass-roots opposition to early attempts at specialization were not limited to Rumania; in Hungary the implementation of a directive allocating the production of radio sets to Bulgaria brought about a short-lived boycott, and resentment was also aroused by the decision to stop producing combines at the EMAG agricultural machinery plant.[86]

Although the original goal of area-wide specialization is frequently reiterated, in practice, bilateral agreements have been the main instruments of cooperation under the umbrella of CEMA. An example of the joint enterprise approach is Haldex, a Hungarian-Polish company established in 1959 in order to apply a Hungarian invention to the processing of Polish coal slack. The availability of cheap hydroelectric power in the Soviet Union led to agreements for Soviet processing of Hungarian bauxite and alumina into aluminum and of isotopes from uranium mined in the Mecsek Mountains; as a *quid pro quo* the Soviet Union undertook in 1957 to assist in the construction of the first Hungarian nuclear power plant at Paks on the Danube south of Budapest, although progress on this project has been very slow.[87] Other joint ventures entered into by Hungary include

[86] *Népszabadság*, March 29, 1963. According to one Hungarian estimate, by 1963 only from 3 to 5 per cent of the area's machinery production conformed with the CEMA specialization directives; see A. Balassa, "The Structure of the Machinery Industry and International Cooperation," *Közgazdasági Szemle*, 11, no. 12 (1964) : 1274.

[87] See Jaroslav G. Polach, "Nuclear Power in East Europe," *East Europe*, 17, no. 5 (1968) : 3–12.

one with Bulgaria for the manufacture of engineering products in the latter country and another, with Poland, for the extraction of phosphate deposits at Kingisepp in the Soviet Union.

In addition, a number of multilateral links have materialized which only indirectly fall under the aegis of CEMA. In 1964 Apró announced that on Hungarian initiative an organization for joint planning in the production and distribution of metallurgical products, Intermetall, had been founded and headquartered in Budapest.[88] By the following year all the East European members of the Communist bloc except Rumania had joined Intermetall; it is worth noting, however, that its supranational character is qualified by the requirement that all its resolutions be unanimous. The Friendship pipeline from the Soviet Union has been supplying Hungary through its Slovakian branch with two thirds of her crude-oil requirements, and plans are afoot to build a second link directly from the Ukraine to the Százhalombatta refinery near Budapest;[89] the construction of the original pipeline had been a joint venture by the beneficiaries, with Hungary contributing most of the communications equipment. Hungary also participates in the system-wide power grid (the international load distributor is located in Prague) and in a joint freight-car pool. The Danubian Commission, whose early history we examined in Chapter 3, has been expanded to include Yugoslavia and Austria, although it too is linked to CEMA through the latter's Permanent Transport Commission, which supervises all aspects of transportation in Eastern Europe; the twentieth anniversary meeting of the Danubian Commission, convened in

88 *Népszabadság,* July 16, 1964.
89 *Magyar Hirlap,* July 28, 1966.

Budapest in March, 1968, was marked by disagree-
ments over a Hungarian-Czech plan to levy a special
toll for improvements and over a Yugoslav-Rumanian
request for system-wide cost-sharing in their Iron Gates
dam project.[90] Finally, the present stage of integration
does not yet encompass a common labor pool as does
the European Economic Community, although in
recent years a special arrangement has sent several
thousand Hungarian *"Gastarbeiter"* to East Germany.

One of the chief stumbling blocks on the road to
economic integration has been the lack of an adequate
multilateral clearing system. Such a system was agreed
upon in principle at the 1957 CEMA meeting in Warsaw, and a certain rationalization of trade practices
did materialize, but the eventual creation in 1964 of
a Bank for Economic Cooperation in Moscow did not
provide an effective means for altering the well-en-
trenched pattern of bilateral relations; even as a credit-
giver, the bank has been limited by the veto power of
every member of its council, and the actual multilateral clearing of trade balances has been insignifi-
cant.[91] Noting these shortcomings, Apró recently called
for the expansion of the bank's clearing and lending
functions, but he conceded that the lack of a convertible currency and a prevailing price system which
is independent of world market conditions and which
maintains prices above world levels hinder progress
toward a fully integrated socialist system.[92]

The evolution of CEMA has been marked by in-

[90] *East Europe,* 17, no. 5 (1968) : 41.

[91] See Henry W. Schaefer, "An East European Payments
Union?" *East Europe,* 15, no. 3 (1966) : 14–21.

[92] Antal Apró, "The Fusion of National and International
Interests in Economic Cooperation among the Socialist States,"
Társadalmi Szemle, 23, no. 12 (1968) : 3–13; cf. Kaser, *Comecon,*
pp. 136–57.

creasingly modest assessments of its functions. Apró noted a few years ago that in practice the coordination of the aims and interests of members who were at different levels of economic development was proving most difficult, and Kádár went so far as to declare in 1966 that "integration to a larger or smaller degree of the economies of the Comecon countries is not planned."[93] The stress is more and more on coordination as distinct from integration, and recent conferences on the issue of specialization have (in keeping with such experiments as the NEM) considered proposals for transferring the responsibility to individual enterprises, although objections were raised that the latter would not necessarily respect the over-all goal of a socialist division of labor.[94] If, as seems likely, such proposals are implemented, CEMA will become irrelevant unless its structures are brought into line with economic realities.[95]

As the system now operates, CEMA countries sign annual trade protocols within the framework of long-term agreements. For Hungary, which is heavily dependent on trade (40 per cent of the national product is exported) and even more heavily dependent on her partners in CEMA, the terms of these agreements represent the alpha and omega of economic survival, and endemic rumors to the effect that the terms of trade (particularly with the Soviet Union) are not always advantageous have given rise to periodic reassurances by party chiefs.[96] Although perfect equality and reci-

[93] Népszabadság, February 13, 1964, and August 1, 1966.

[94] See Figyelő, May 11, 1966.

[95] See Michael Gamarnikow, "Is Comecon Obsolete?" East Europe, 18, no. 4 (1968) : 12–18.

[96] Antal Apró, "On Hungarian-Soviet Economic Cooperation," Társadalmi Szemle, 22, no. 11 (1967) : 17–25; cf. Kaser, Comecon, pp. 144–45.

procity in trade relations with Russia are not likely to prevail, it must be noted that CEMA does offer Hungary a protected market for the output of her relatively inefficient industries. Attempts have been made within the framework of the NEM to improve Hungary's competitive position in international trade; individual enterprises now have more freedom to make trade deals (although most still work through the state foreign trade agencies), and "foreign-currency multipliers" are used as an incentive to boost exports. Nevertheless, in addition to the more intangible political influences, there are concrete economic factors which contribute to the orientation of Hungary's trade toward CEMA; briefly, these are a shortage of raw materials, a surplus of machinery production, an inability to compete on world markets except in agricultural produce, due to low productivity, and a lack of hard currency. To these factors must be added the necessity of maintaining a standard of living higher than that prevailing in the Soviet Union. One of Hungary's foremost economists, József Bognár, has been particularly vocal in urging that the domestic economy strive to approximate world market norms through the acceleration of technological development, the encouragement of competition by individual industries for markets within as well as outside the CEMA sphere, and the introduction of convertible currencies; Bognár also recommended cooperative ventures with Western industries on the enterprise level to boost productivity and exports.[97]

Recent developments provide evidence of Hungary's

---

[97] Jósef Bognár, "Principles of Foreign Trade in the New Economic Mechanism," *New Hungarian Quarterly*, 8, no. 26 (1967) : 156–71; cf. Béla Csikós-Nagy, "Socialist Economic Theory and the New Mechanism," *ibid.*, no. 28 (1967) : 52.

search for extra-CEMA ventures and markets. Despite frequent complaints about the European Economic Community's trade restrictions,[98] trade agreements have been signed with several West European countries, and in 1968 Hungary reached its first formal agreement with the EEC covering the export of slaughter pigs; for the time being, foodstuffs appear to be the main source of exports to that area, notably to Italy. Within the last two years the Hungarian National Bank has opened branches in London, Paris, and Zurich, contracts for local production have been signed with Western firms such as Coca-Cola and British Ford, an enterprise called Geominco has been set up to prospect for and import raw materials (presumably from underdeveloped countries), and a fifteen million Eurodollar loan has been negotiated for the development of Hungary's aluminum-processing industry. Trade with Yugoslavia is still well below prewar levels, but a Mixed Committee for Economic Cooperation is now in operation, and in 1968 a bilateral agreement was signed associating Hungarian and Yugoslav financial institutions in a banking consortium; another joint venture, by Czech, Hungarian, and Yugoslav oil concerns, aims at the construction of a pipeline from the Adriatic to bring in Iranian oil and supplement the declining Soviet surplus.

This search for new markets is yet to be reflected in trade statistics. Although the total value of Hungary's trade has doubled since 1960, distribution by markets has remained relatively stable, with the CEMA system accounting for roughly two-thirds of her trade; in 1967 the Soviet Union alone took 36.1 per cent of her exports and supplied 33.3 per cent of her imports, followed in order of importance by East Germany,

[98] See *Magyar Hirlap,* June 12, 1968.

Czechoslovakia, and Poland.[99] Hungary's reliance on CEMA is even more striking in certain product categories. In 1965 CEMA's share of her exports (imports) stood at 87 per cent (80 per cent) for heavy machinery, 53 per cent (62 per cent) for raw materials, 67 per cent (69 per cent) for manufactured consumer goods, and 50 per cent (34 per cent) for foodstuffs.[100] Of the imports, 95.1 per cent of the iron ore, 50.9 per cent of the rolled steel, 45.6 per cent of the raw wool, 78.4 per cent of the lumber, and 55.7 per cent of the newsprint originated in the Soviet Union in 1967;[101] the same country takes a substantial proportion of Hungary's output of raw materials, textiles, machinery, and foodstuffs. In the West the German Federal Republic is Hungary's best trading partner (with approximately 5 per cent of the trade total), followed by Italy, Austria, the United Kingdom, and France; all of these provide important markets for meat and agricultural produce. It is clear from these statistics that, in terms of the volume of trade, Hungary is highly integrated into, and dependent upon, the socialist bloc. According to the criteria of cooperation, specialization, and joint planning, however, this state of integration remains heavily qualified by both present practices and secular centrifugal trends.

Political Integration and the
Socialist Commonwealth

Since 1955 the Warsaw Treaty Organization has been the primary institution for military and political

[99] *MSZ, 1968,* pp. 96–97.

[100] *Handbook of Hungarian Foreign Trade* (Budapest, 1967), p. 26. For a commodity breakdown of Hungary's foreign trade, see the appendix, tables 8 and 10.

[101] *MSZ, 1968,* pp. 100–108.

coordination in the socialist system. Direction of military affairs is highly centralized in Moscow and is functionally indistinguishable from the operations of the Soviet General Staff (nominally each minister of defense is a deputy commander-in-chief of the joint forces),[102] although the passive role played by Rumania on the occasion of the police action in Czechoslovakia indicates that political considerations may conceivably nullify such direction. Speaking at a meeting of the Political Consultative Committee in 1958, Kádár declared that Soviet intervention to crush the "counterrevolution" had been required by the terms of the treaty, which guaranteed the defense of the socialist peoples' peace and freedom;[103] earlier, on May 27, 1957, a new Status of Forces Agreement had been signed which regularized the temporary stationing of Soviet forces in Hungary.[104] Almost every subsequent Soviet-Hungarian conference has given rise to rumors of an impending evacuation, and in March, 1958, just prior to Khrushchev's visit to Hungary, some 17,000 troops were ceremonially withdrawn; but on that occasion the authorities took great pains to warn "counterrevolutionary elements" that this should not be interpreted as a weakening of the Kádár regime.[105]

At present, four Soviet divisions as well as some air units, totalling approximately 80,000 men, are stationed in Hungary,[106] and it is likely that the cost of

[102] See Raymond L. Garthoff, "The Military Establishment," *East Europe*, 14, no. 9 (1965) : 2–16.

[103] Grzybowski, *Socialist Commonwealth of Nations*, p. 201.

[104] For the text, see United Nations, *Report of the Special Committee on the Problem of Hungary*, pp. 60–62.

[105] Sándor Kiss, "Soviet Troops in Hungary," *East Europe*, 13, no. 10 (1964) : 8–13.

[106] Institute of Strategic Studies, *The Military Balance, 1968–1969* (London, 1968), p. 6.

their upkeep is borne by their hosts. Supervised by Soviet "advisers," Hungary's own military establishment underwent yet another process of purification and reorganization after the revolution, and about the only concession made to national sentiment was the introduction of a more indigenous style of uniform. Military expenditures rose to 7.4 per cent of the budget for fiscal 1963 in response to the Berlin crisis, then fell to 4.6 per cent in 1968, and current estimates show that in terms of her gross national product Hungary spends less on defense (2.6 per cent in 1967) than any other member of the bloc, while only Rumania and Bulgaria have a lower defense expenditure per capita.[107] In terms of manpower the regular armed forces, numbering 102,000, are also the smallest in the bloc; to this must be added the paramilitary forces, notably 35,000 security troops and border guards and a workers' militia of more than 100,000 men.[108] One can only surmise that Hungary's relative military weakness is a product both of economic priorities and of a lingering mistrust in Moscow arising from the behavior of the Hungarian armed forces during the revolution.

In addition to her continuing membership in the Warsaw Pact, Hungary renewed the largely symbolic twenty-year treaties of friendship, cooperation, and mutual assistance with the Soviet Union and the German Democratic Republic in 1967 and with Poland and Czechoslovakia in 1968; other, more functional manifestations of a socialist community include the creation of Intervision in 1963—a television network

[107] *Ibid.,* pp. 3, 55.

[108] The strength of the army stands at 95,000 men (one tank division, five motorized rifle divisions), that of the air force at 7,000 men (140 combat aircraft), while the navy consists of a Danube flotilla of fifteen vessels and a training ship (*ibid.,* p. 3).

linking the Soviet Union and all the East European states except Yugoslavia—and of Photo International in 1965, which links the Hungarian, Soviet, Czech, Polish, and East German news agencies. Finally, in order to rationalize legal procedures, Hungary has signed legal aid treaties with every European socialist state except Albania, and has concluded dual nationality conventions with the Soviet Union (1957), Bulgaria (1958), Czechoslovakia (1960), and Poland (1961).[109]

All these structures and formal links, however, provide only an imperfect image of Hungary's political position within the socialist system and of the Hungarian Socialist Workers' Party's relations with her sister parties in the bloc. More than any other communist leader, Kádár had been Khrushchev's man, and the latter's fall in 1964 obviously came as a shock to him, but by and large the Hungarian leadership has been consistent in its pursuit of a centrist course that deviates only marginally from the international policies of the CPSU. In the Rumanian-integrationist conflict Hungary refrained from openly condemning the Bucharest regime and, as we saw earlier, adjusted herself readily to the decentralization within CEMA and to the stress on coordination instead of integration. Concerning the Sino-Soviet schism, the regime took a more definite stand by voicing concurrence with the CPSU's open letter to the Chinese in March, 1963, but it did not initially repeat the Soviet call for an international conference of all parties to discuss the matter;[110] it is worth noting that in order to forestall internal polycentrist elements, Kállai warned against any interpretation of the schism as offering new oppor-

[109] See Grzybowski, *Socialist Commonwealth of Nations,* pp. 9–16.

[110] *Népszabadság,* July 16, 1963.

tunities for a "third road" for Hungary.[111] Trade with China dwindled after the split, a mutual expulsion of students occurred in 1966, and, when in the following year Peking mobs attacked the Hungarian ambassador's automobile, the regime denounced Mao's Cultural Revolution in no uncertain terms.[112] Hungary's alignment with Moscow was never in question; Kádár, speaking at the Twenty-third Congress of the CPSU in March, 1966, asserted emphatically that there could be no such thing as anti-Soviet communism.

Recent developments within the Communist bloc serve to underline Kádár's calculated allegiance to Moscow as well as his inclination to liberalize cautiously and to moderate interparty conflicts. At the United Nations, Hungary invariably supports the Soviet Union, and she has followed Moscow's lead in providing North Vietnam with financial and technical assistance. The Czechoslovak crisis that developed early in 1968 placed Kádár in a mediating role which may not have been entirely prescribed by the Soviet leadership. When the consultative meeting to plan a world communist conference (convened in Budapest in February, 1968) broke up over the issue of the criticism of individual parties with the exit of Rumania's delegation, the Hungarians remained true to Moscow's line. As the Czech apostasy gained momentum, however, Kádár met secretly with Dubček on several occasions—before the Warsaw conference of the eventual invaders, before the Soviet-Czech confrontation at Cierna, and just before the invasion—presumably to warn the latter of impending disaster and to suggest certain compromises. The original Hungarian position was that the Czechoslovaks were fighting the same

[111] *Ibid.,* June 25, 1964.
[112] MTI release, January 30, 1967.

two-front battle—against extreme sectarians and bourgeois revisionists—that Hungary had faced in 1956 and that they would be well advised to profit from that experience; a pro-Nagy article which appeared in *Literární Listy* in June elicited bitter comments.[113] Nevertheless, once Moscow decided to put into effect what became known as the "Brezhnev doctrine," the Kádár regime dutifully fell in line with the other interventionist parties. Hungary's participation in the invasion caused widespread dismay, not only among the public but also in the armed forces, and the Magyar population of Slovakia was reportedly less than enthusiastic in its welcome; conversely, the Dubček regime reserved for Hungary's action an understanding that it did not extend to the other invaders.

Public sympathy in Hungary for Dubček's efforts at liberalization prompted official denials that the Hungarian Communist Party would change its course, and assertions that the Hungarian model of economic reform was a shining example of the adaptation of Marxism-Leninism to national conditions. It is nonetheless significant that a number of intellectuals (including Hegedüs) were merely "reprimanded" for openly criticizing Hungary's participation in the invasion, and that Premier Fock felt the need to argue that the international nature of the intervention had precluded a preliminary assessment of public opinion.[114]

In its relations with the West, the Kádár regime has been guided by its desire for recognition and legitimacy. Agreements on closer cultural and economic relations were signed by Foreign Minister János Péter on the occasion of his visit to Paris in 1965, diplomatic relations with the United States have been upgraded,

[113] *Népszabadság*, June 27, 1968.
[114] *East Europe*, 18, no. 2 (1969) : 45–46.

and a certain *modus vivendi* has been reached with the Vatican; in keeping with the Soviet Union's own policies, the tentative rapprochement with Bonn is still limited to increased economic contacts. In September, 1964, Tito made his first official visit to Hungary since his break with Stalin, but Hungarian-Yugoslav relations were set back by the Czech invasion, and the Hungarians boycotted the subsequent Ninth Congress of the Yugoslav Communist Party.

An enduring obstacle to political integration within the socialist system has been the multiplicity of ethnic and territorial disputes, and the half-century-old question of Hungarian minorities has plagued relations among the states of the Danubian basin.[115] In Czechoslovakia the Magyar minority, after being subjected to widespread discrimination and deportations in the Stal nist period, acquired recognition as a separate natic nality group in the 1960 constitution; but, despite cultural concessions, it enjoys a low socioeconomic status, and the new federal structure, a response to Slovakian nationalism, is unlikely to bring about an improvement. Yugoslavia's nationalities policies have legalized the ethnic status and cultural rights of Hungarians living in the Voivodina, and Hungarians remain the most nationalistic Yugoslav minority.[116] In Rumania the trend has been in the other direction. The 1952 constitution created a Hungarian autonomous province to ensure the cultural survival of the

[115] See István Révay, "Hungarian Minorities under Communist Rule," in *Facts About Hungary*, ed. Imre Kovács, (New York, 1966), pp. 288–300; cf. George A. Schöpflin, "National Minorities under Communism in Eastern Europe," in *Eastern Europe in Transition*, ed. Kurt London (Baltimore, 1966), pp. 117–41.

[116] See Paul Shoup, "Yugoslavia's National Minorities Under Communism," *Slavic Review*, 22, no. 1 (1963) : 68, 78, 80–81.

one-and-a-half million Magyars and Szeklers in Transylvania, but after 1958 the growing nationalism of the Rumanian leaders led to deportations, a curtailment of most minority rights, and the abolition of many educational institutions, including the independent Bólyai University at Cluj (Kolozsvár), so that by 1962 all schools were integrated.[117] Subsequently the county system was reorganized to fragment the minority, while administrative measures were aimed at reducing the proportion of Hungarians in the towns and cities. Magyar minorities throughout Eastern Europe had reacted enthusiastically to the 1956 revolution, and that reassertion of national consciousness only strengthened the determination of the Bucharest regime to employ all available means to assimilate the former into a Rumanian national and linguistic collectivity.

Since Marxist theory views nationalism as an aberration intimately linked with imperialism,[118] the Hungarian government has had little option to act as the defender of the rights of Magyar minorities, but in view of the widespread popular concern for the latter there has prevailed a remarkable silence in official circles and in the press regarding this issue. The façade of comradely relations with sister parties has been maintained, although in the case of Hungary and Rumania a minor cold war can be observed; trade has stagnated, visas are still required for travel between the two countries, and only recently has an agreement

[117] See Ferenc A. Váli, "Transylvania and the Hungarian Minority," pp. 32–44; cf. J. F. Brown, "Rumania Today, I: Towards 'Integration,'" *Problems of Communism,* 18, no. 1 (1969) : 12, 16.

[118] See Zoltán Komócsin, "Patriotism, National Interests, Internationalism," *World Marxist Review,* 9, no. 6 (1966): 33–38.

been reached to raise the annual tourist flow to 100,000 from its previous ceiling of 70,000. Both Komócsin and Kádár have made veiled references to the minority problem, but evidently the Hungarian leaders feel that any encouragement of nationalism—whether Magyar or Rumanian—would jeopardize their own position.[119]

The persistence of national consciousness among Magyar minorities may well have been one of the stimuli behind the Kádár regime's official advocacy of Danubian cooperation, a foreign-policy orientation which has been in evidence since Péter's visits to Paris and Vienna and the popularization of General de Gaulle's vision of a reorganized *"Europe des patries"* from the Atlantic to the Urals. With increasing frequency Kádár has noted in his speeches that, while Hungary's membership in the socialist camp predetermined her relations with other states, geographical concepts retain a certain validity.[120] According to this policy, as outlined by Foreign Minister Péter and others, Western Europe must turn to the East to reduce its economic dependence on the United States, and "cooperation among the Danubian countries, especially those situated along the line dividing the two social systems, may become a factor of considerable value in furthering the development of a European organization of peace and security."[121] A prominent Hungarian

119 See Gabriel Fischer, "Nationalism and Internationalism in Hungary and Rumania," *Canadian Slavonic Papers*, 10, no. 1 (1968) : 26–41.

120 *Népszabadság*, February 12, 1965, and February 23, 1966.

121 János Péter, "Hungary and Europe," *New Hungarian Quarterly*, 8, no. 25 (1967) : 14–19. Added Péter: "Even today international reaction is trying to exploit the Treaty of Trianon, dictated to Hungary by the imperialist powers, in order to stir up trouble among the peoples of the Danube basin." On

publicist, Tibor Pethő, averred that Czechoslovakia, Hungary, Yugoslavia, and Austria form a particularly promising nucleus for cooperation, since among the first three there exists a trend "towards still greater cooperation and the gradual reduction in the importance of national frontiers," while the relationship between them and Austria is the "keystone of peaceful coexistence in the Danube Valley."[122]

These Hungarian initiatives have up to now met with little positive response from within the Communist bloc, a fact which has led commentators to dismiss the likelihood that Soviet designs on Austria lie behind the policy.[123] It is conceivable that Kádár's Danubian orientation represents a regionalism which is part of the small-power syndrome, as well as a search for new markets and economies of scale; one tangible outcome of Hungary's rapprochement with Austria was an agreement, signed in April, 1965, for the exchange of electrical power. This precedent for East-West cooperation has not been reaffirmed, however, and the invasion of Czechoslovakia offered a reminder that the requirements of ideological orthodoxy will almost invariably outweigh regional or particularistic considerations. By the same token, one can safely assume that any loosening of Soviet hegemony over Eastern Europe will precipitate, for better or for worse, a reassertion of historical and geographical realities.

another occasion, addressing the National Assembly before it ratified the second twenty-year Soviet-Hungarian treaty of friendship, cooperation, and mutual assistance, Péter included the Ruthenians (and, by inference, the Magyars living in the Carpatho-Ukraine) among the "Danubian peoples"; see *Népszabadság*, December 21, 1967.

[122] Tibor Pethő, "Modern Forms of Cooperation in the Danube Valley," *New Hungarian Quarterly*, 8, no. 27 (1967): 10–16.

[123] See Charles András, "The Slow Drift to Danubian Cooperation," *East Europe*, 17, no. 12 (1968): 24–25.

6: TRENDS AND PROSPECTS

Were geographic proximity the dominant stimulus toward regional integration, East Europe would long ago have coalesced into a cohesive and powerful entity. Instead, its history has been marked by periodic fragmentations and realignments and by shifts in the spheres of influence of great powers lying to the West and to the East. The question under consideration is whether at the present stage of their development the Eastern Europeans have indeed created a community marked by, in the words of one political scientist, "high intra-group homogeneity, clear qualitative differences from nearby states outside the groups, and . . . distinct transaction boundaries."[1]

In the political sphere, integration has progressed *integratio* to the point where institutional uniformity and a certain homogeneity of the official value systems prevail. The evolution of the social structure has followed a similar pattern, from the initial atomization to the current new forms of stratification. On the other hand, the mass belief systems are still differentiated by national heritage and have responded

---

[1] Bruce M. Russett, *International Regions and the International System* (Chicago, 1967), p. 168.

only marginally to the transnational ideology propounded by communist parties.

In the realm of economic integration, the realignment of trade links has created the outlines of a community, but one in which the coordination of certain economic functions has not overcome particularistic tendencies and has not led to consensual system-wide cooperation. While the prevailing trade patterns may have occasioned a degree of habitual dependence within the Soviet bloc, the inequality of the units and the leverage exerted by the Soviet Union by virtue of its size have inhibited the development of genuine interdependence or a community of interests. The decentralizing reforms of the last few years are likely to retard further economic integration, at least within the present institutional structures.

Some characteristics of the Hungarian system are shared by her partners in the bloc; others are the product of indigenous factors. The imposition of a Marxist-Leninist belief system, either by force in the Rákosi era or by gentler persuasion since 1960, has demonstrably failed. The intelligentsia is no longer a willing channel for indoctrination, while the emerging middle classes appear to embody a mixture of socialistic and secular values that to some extent transcend both state and systemic boundaries, but that at the same time are qualified by a strong national consciousness. One of the critical problems confronting the regime has been the growing irrelevance of the Communist Party, in the ideological sense, as the sole aggregator of demands and the only agent of change; Kádár will be finding it increasingly difficult to accommodate pluralistic pressures within his self-imposed pragmatic ethos without abdicating the leading role of the party.

The Hungarian political system vis à vis the Soviet

Union is highly permeable and penetrated, its autonomy being circumscribed closely, although in a less overt manner than was the norm under Stalin. The regime derives a tangible benefit from the present state of integration, for its maintenance remains in large measure dependent upon the proximity, power, and interests of the Soviet Union. For the Hungarian people, the marginal economic benefits of membership are outweighed by the constraints placed on internal liberalization, on a more open identification with the Western cultural and political tradition, and on an independent and probably neutral international orientation. Nevertheless, being strategically indefensible and economically weak, Hungary would not be in a position to move toward secession even if this was envisaged by her leaders. Both internally and on the systemic level, Kádár lacks the power to implement a voluntaristic foreign policy, and the precedents of Imre Nagy and Dubček demonstrated that too close an identification of the regime with national and particularistic interests is an invitation to disaster. Popular awareness of this dilemma in turn has brought about a certain consensus among the élite and the population at large that Hungary can afford no provocation of the Soviet Union, and this consensus lies at the root of the regime's tenuous legitimacy. Within this conjuncture, Kádár's perfomance as a self-appointed agent of compromise in external as well as internal affairs can be viewed as a product both of his determination to demonstrate that the party can provide responsive and popular government and of his perception that this can be accomplished throughout the system only by quiet diplomacy and an attenuation of the forces of nationalism.

The East Europeans' common experience with

twenty years of Soviet suzerainty has created regional bonds that to some extent overshadow historical rivalries, while the requirements of economic development may in the long run bring about joint action to achieve economies of scale. Yet Rumania's economic nationalism, Bulgaria's irredentist interest in Yugoslav Macedonia, Polish apprehensions regarding the permanence of the Oder-Neisse frontier, and the Hungarians' concern for the fate of Magyar minorities indicate that integration has not resolved all conflicts of national interest. History shows that such a resolution can be enduring only when arrived at through cooperation that is free from the interference of the Great Powers.

For the time being the *ultima ratio* of integration is Soviet power and the determination of the Kremlin to wield it in defense of bloc unity. In East Berlin, in Hungary, in Czechoslovakia, Stalin's successors have repeatedly resorted to the use of force to prevent disintegration, which they defined as any challenge to the monopoly of the Communist Party, any internal reform that deviates significantly from the Soviet pattern, and, of course, any drift toward unilateral disengagement and neutralism. The necessity for such extreme measures indicates that, whatever the theoretical advantages of a regional community, integration on Soviet terms was never the product of a system-wide consensus.

It might be argued that the immoderate use of force is likely to be self-defeating by reinforcing disintegrative tendencies, but in the case of Eastern Europe this hypothesis can have only long-range significance. The Soviet Union has employed other tactics before resorting to force—one suggestion has been that it is using Transylvania as a bait to keep the Hungarians in line and to intimidate the Rumanians—and the rapidly deteriorating Sino-Soviet relations may postpone initiatives toward further integration. Nevertheless, the twilight of empires tends to be marked internally by rigidity and spasms of unprecedented violence, while on the global scale the increasingly symbiotic relationship of the Soviet Union and the United States appears to preclude any external threat to the former's sphere of influence in Eastern Europe.

APPENDIX: SELECTED DATA TABLES

TABLE 1
Population Growth, 1920–67

Year	Total Population	Live Deaths (per 1,000)	Births (per 1,000)	Natural Increase (per 1,000)	Infant Mortality[1]
1920[2]	7,986,875	21.8[3]	21.7[3]	0.1[3]	194.8[3]
1930[4]	8,685,109	26.0[5]	17.0[5]	9.0[5]	172.2[5]
1941[6]	9,316,074	19.9[7]	14.1[7]	5.8[7]	131.1[7]
1949[8]	9,204,799	20.6	11.4	9.2	91.0
1950	9,293,000	20.9	11.4	9.5	85.7
1951	9,383,000	20.2	11.7	8.5	83.9
1952	9,463,000	19.6	11.3	8.3	69.9
1953	9,545,000	21.6	11.7	9.9	70.8
1954	9,645,000	23.0	11.0	12.0	60.7
1955	9,767,000	21.4	10.0	11.4	60.0
1956	9,883,000	19.5	10.5	9.0	58.8
1957	9,829,000	17.0	10.5	6.5	63.1
1958	9,850,000	16.0	9.9	6.1	58.1
1959	9,913,000	15.2	10.5	4.7	52.4
1960[9]	9,961,044	14.7	10.2	4.5	47.6
1961	10,005,980	14.0	9.6	4.4	44.1
1962	10,049,935	12.9	10.8	2.1	47.9
1963	10,071,715	13.1	9.9	3.2	42.9
1964	10,104,179	13.1	10.0	3.1	40.0
1965	10,135,490	13.1	10.7	2.4	38.8
1966	10,160,380	13.6	10.0	3.6	38.4
1967	10,196,926	14.6	10.7	3.9	37.0

[1] Per 1,000 live births.
[2] Census, December 31, 1920.
[3] Average for 1916–20.
[4] Census, December 31, 1930.
[5] Average for 1926–30.
[6] Census, January 31, 1941.
[7] Average for 1936–40.
[8] Census, January 1, 1949. Figures for subsequent years are for January 1.
[9] Census, January 1, 1960.
Sources: Központi Statisztikai Hivatal, *Statisztikai évkönyv, 1966* (Budapest, 1967), and Hungarian Central Statistical Office, *Statistical Yearbook, 1967* (Budapest, 1968).

189

TABLE 2
Distribution of Population by Age Group and Sex, 1920–67

Year	Under 15	15–39	40–59	60 and Over
1920	30.6%	41.3%	19.1%	9.0%
1930	27.5	42.6	20.1	9.8
1941	26.0	40.6	22.7	10.7
1949	24.9	38.8	24.7	11.6
1960	25.4	36.8	24.0	13.8
1965	23.6	36.2	24.7	15.5
1966	23.0	36.3	24.9	15.8
1967	22.5	36.4	25.0	16.1
Male	23.9	37.3	24.4	14.4
Female	21.3	35.4	25.5	17.7

Source: Központi Statisztikai Hivatal, Magyar statisztikai zsebkönyv, 1968 (Budapest, 1968).

TABLE 3
Distribution of Manpower, 1960 and 1967

	1960 (thousands)	1967 (thousands)
Total Population	9,961	10,197
Industry		
State	1,142	1,361
Cooperative	161	207
Private	81	61
Total	1,384	1,629
Building Industry		
State	239	267
Cooperative	25	44
Private	22	23
Total	286	334
Agriculture		
State	291	272
Cooperative	727	685
Total	1,018	957
Transportation and Communications	287	308
Trade		
State	207	249
Cooperative	74	98
Private	11	10
Total	292	357
Other Occupations	630.9	786.9
Total Active Labor Force	3,897.9	4,371.9

Source: Hungarian Central Statistical Office, *Statistical Yearbook, 1967.*

TABLE 4
Selected Industrial Indices, 1960–67

Year	Gross Production	Employment	Productivity	Mining	Electrical Industry	Metallurgy	Engineering	Chemicals	Light Industry	Food Processing
1960	100	100	100	100	100	100	100	100	100	100
1961	110	102	108	107	109	108	114	120	109	110
1962	119	105	113	111	119	116	127	136	115	118
1963	127	109	117	121	129	121	136	151	122	128
1964	138	112	123	127	142	127	148	170	132	140
1965	145	113	129	130	153	130	157	189	138	143
1966	154	114	135	134	167	139	170	213	146	148
1967	168	118	143	132	182	148	187	242	160	159

Source: Hungarian Central Statistical Office, *Statistical Yearbook, 1967.*

TABLE 5
Agricultural Indices, 1961–67

Year	Gross Production	Plant Cultivation	Animal Husbandry
		(Average for 1956–60 = 100)	
1961	104	97	109
1962	106	101	109
1963	111	109	110
1964	117	112	122
1965	110	105	117
1966	120	117	122
1967	121	118	125

Source: Hungarian Central Statistical Office, *Statistical Yearbook, 1967.*

TABLE 6
Agricultural Productivity, Selected Crops, 1956–67

Crop	Average, 1956–60	Average, 1961–65	1966	1967
		(Average yield, quintals per hectare)		
Wheat	15.0	18.6	21.6	25.8
Rye	11.4	10.8	11.0	11.0
Barley	17.9	18.7	18.7	20.9
Oats	14.1	11.6	11.9	15.6
Maize	23.1	26.1	31.6	28.5
Sugar beet	212.0	246.4	330.6	324.1
Sunflower seeds	11.0	9.6	10.8	9.6
Potatoes	104.6	79.1	122.8	89.4

Source: Hungarian Central Statistical Office, *Statistical Yearbook, 1967.*

TABLE 7
Balance of Trade, 1921–67

Year	Imports	Exports	Aggregate	Balance
		(millions of pengős)		
1921–25	680.0	516.9	1,196.9	− 163.1
1926–30	1,044.3	892.1	1,936.4	− 152.2
1931–35	385.6	430.4	816.0	+ 44.8
1936–40	484.6	546.7	1,031.3	+ 62.1
1941–45	910.4	1,045.9	1,956.3	+ 135.5
		(millions of forints)		
1946–50	2,177.5	2,108.4	4,285.9	− 69.1
1951	4,625.6	4,645.8	9,271.4	+ 20.2
1952	5,393.9	5,143.2	10,537.1	− 250.7
1953	5,722.3	5,849.0	11,571.3	+ 126.7
1954	6,240.8	6,095.5	12,336.3	− 145.3
1955	6,506.5	7,055.4	13,561.9	+ 548.9
1956	5,648.7	5,716.5	11,365.2	+ 67.8
1957	8,011.3	5,728.3	13,739.6	− 2,283.0
1958	7,407.0	8,024.7	15,431.7	+ 617.7
1959	9,308.6	9,034.8	18,343.4	− 273.8
1960	11,455.4	10,259.8	21,715.2	− 1,195.6
1961	12,039.6	12,079.6	24,119.2	+ 40.0
1962	13,485.2	12,905.5	26,390.7	− 579.7
1963	15,326.7	14,155.5	29,482.2	− 1,171.2
1964	17,546.0	15,869.8	33,415.8	− 1,676.2
1965	17,848.5	17,721.3	35,569.8	− 127.2
1966	18,378.5	18,705.1	37,083.6	+ 326.6
1967	20,841.4	19,971.2	40,812.6	− 870.2

Source: Hungarian Central Statistical Office, *Statistical Yearbook, 1967.*

TABLE 8
Commodity Structure of Foreign Trade, 1938–67
(Percentages)

Product	1938	1950	1960	1967
	Imports			
Machines, vehicles, capital goods	10.6	22.0	27.8	32.3
Industrial consumer goods	8.8	1.5	5.0	6.4
Raw materials and semifinished products	73.1	72.7	58.9	52.8
Food products	7.5	3.8	8.3	8.5
	Exports			
Machines, vehicles, capital goods	9.3	23.0	38.0	31.1
Industrial consumer goods	10.2	20.3	17.8	23.1
Raw materials and semifinished products	23.5	17.5	23.6	23.9
Food products	57.0	39.2	20.6	21.9

Source: Központi Statisztikai Hivatal, *Magyar statisztikai zsebkönyv, 1968.*

TABLE 9
Foreign Trade with Selected Countries, 1938–67
(Percentages)

Country	1938	1950	1960	1967
		Imports		
Bulgaria	0.8	2.0	1.3	2.2
Czechoslovakia	6.7	10.3	11.5	8.6
Poland	1.4	9.9	5.1	6.3
Rumania	9.8	7.0	4.3	2.2
Soviet Union	0.1	24.5	31.0	33.3
Yugoslavia	4.5	0.0	2.1	1.8
Germany, East	} 30.1	2.6	10.3	10.9
Germany, West		9.9	5.7	5.8
Austria	11.5	5.7	3.5	3.6
United Kingdom	6.3	3.5	3.2	3.2
France	1.5	1.5	2.6	2.0
Netherlands	3.7	2.7	1.3	0.8
Italy	6.3	2.9	2.7	3.1
Switzerland	2.5	3.9	1.3	2.4
United States	5.3	1.8	0.2	0.5
		Exports		
Bulgaria	1.0	1.4	0.7	0.6
Czechoslovakia	4.1	10.6	10.7	9.0
Poland	1.0	8.2	5.2	6.0
Rumania	4.0	7.7	3.0	2.2
Soviet Union	0.1	28.9	29.3	36.1
Yugoslavia	3.0	0.0	4.3	1.8
Germany, East	} 27.4	7.4	11.5	9.6
Germany, West		7.4	5.1	4.3
Austria	18.3	5.2	3.7	2.8
United Kingdom	8.1	0.1	2.0	2.3
France	1.9	1.1	1.6	1.4
Netherlands	1.6	2.1	1.3	1.1
Italy	8.5	3.4	2.4	4.9
Switzerland	3.2	3.7	2.3	2.7
United States	2.4	0.7	0.3	0.3

Source: Központi Statisztikai Hivatal, *Magyar statisztikai zsebkönyv, 1968.*

TABLE 10
Foreign Trade by Commodity Group and Area, 1967
(Percentages)

Product		Socialist Countries (including Cuba)	Rest of World
Fuels, electrical energy	Import	98.5	1.5
	Export	28.6	71.4
Raw materials and semifinished products	Import	60.6	39.4
	Export	61.3	38.7
Machines, vehicles, capital goods	Import	76.8	23.2
	Export	93.6	6.4
Industrial consumer goods	Import	80.3	19.7
	Export	72.2	27.8
Food products	Import	42.7	57.3
	Export	48.5	51.5
Aggregate	Import	66.6	33.4
	Export	68.6	31.4

Source: Hungarian Central Statistical Office, Statistical Yearbook, 1967.

SELECTED BIBLIOGRAPHY

Aczél, Tamás, and Méray, Tibor. *The Revolt of the Mind.* New York and London: Praeger, 1960.

Brzezinski, Zbigniew K. *The Soviet Bloc.* Cambridge, Mass.: Harvard University Press, 1967.

Fejtő, François. "Hungarian Communism." In *Communism in Europe,* ed. William E. Griffith. Cambridge, Mass.: M.I.T. Press, 1964.

Grzybowski, Kazimierz. *The Socialist Commonwealth of Nations.* New Haven, Conn.: Yale University Press, 1964.

Helmreich, Ernst C., ed. *Hungary.* New York: Praeger, 1957.

Kaser, Michael. *Comecon.* London: Oxford University Press, 1965.

Kecskeméti, Paul. *The Unexpected Revolution.* Stanford, Calif.: Stanford University Press, 1961.

Kovács, Imre, ed. *Facts About Hungary.* New York: The Hungarian Committee, 1966.

Lasky, Melvin J., ed. *The Hungarian Revolution: A White Book.* New York: Praeger, 1957.

Macartney, C. A. *Hungary: A Short History.* Chicago: Aldine Press, 1962.

Macartney, C. A. *October Fifteenth: A History of Modern Hungary, 1929–1945.* 2 vols. Edinburgh: Edinburgh University Press, 1956–57.

Skilling, H. Gordon. *The Governments of Communist East Europe.* New York: Crowell, 1966.

Váli, Ferenc A. *Rift and Revolt in Hungary.* Cambridge, Mass.: Harvard University Press, 1961.

Zinner, Paul E. *Revolution in Hungary.* New York: Columbia University Press, 1962.

INDEX

F1